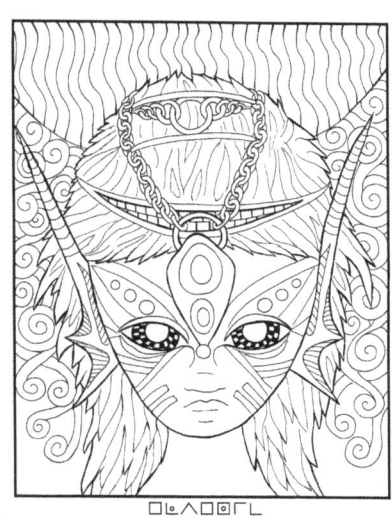

Mini Fantasy Flip Faces

POCKET-SIZED
OPTICAL ILLUSIONS COLORING BOOK

'TRICK SLATTERY

COLOR ARTIST:

Mini Fantasy Flip Faces
POCKET-SIZED
Optical Illusions Coloring Book

Published in 2017 by

Tricksplace

ISBN: 978-0-9938669-4-4

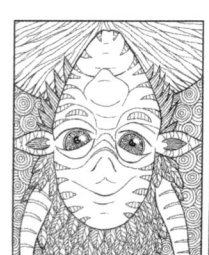 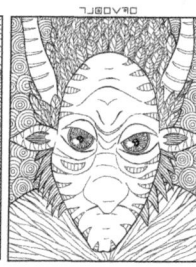 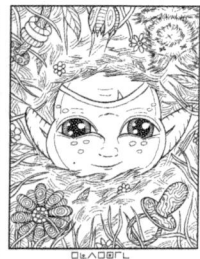 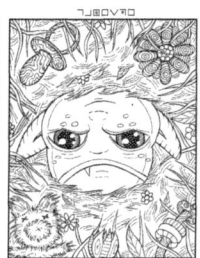

 Created by 'Trick Slattery
www.TricksPlace.com

Thank you for helping Terraflippia! Enjoy your coloring.

All illustrations can be seen in two ways with a "flip". I've created them with varying complexities, so if you are looking for a challenge you can choose a more intricate drawing with lots of nooks to color or if you are looking for something quick and easy, a more simplistic page would be the way to go.

Each of the 25 hand drawn entirely original illustrations has been duplicated for a total of 50 coloring pages (the duplicates are in the back half of the book), giving you a chance to color a different "view" of the same artwork or for a do-over.

Though the illustrations are single-sided, you will still want to protect the pages under the one you are working with. Slide a blank sheet of paper between the page you are coloring and the next image underneath it. This will help protect the other pages from hard colored pencil indents, etc. If you use markers or gel pens you may want to use more than one page, or cardstock, as wet media may seep through to the next page.

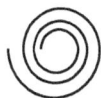

SHARE YOUR COLORED WORK!
After you have colored in a page - scan it in and share it on social media with the hashtag of #tricksplace and #fantasyflipcoloring. Please do not post or share uncolored pages. Also, join this dedicated facebook group and share there: facebook.com/groups/TricksPlaceColoring/

There is an invisible world that humans cannot see called Terraflippia. It is a world filled with magic, elves, fairies, wizards, goblins, trolls, and other fantasy creatures.

This world is a beautiful world, but it is also one that is divided. The two main factions of the world are the Elvenic and the Ganespe. The Elvenic consists of elves and various allies such as the grand wizard and the unicorns. The Ganespe consists of goblins, trolls, imps, and other alliance members. This division between factions has caused great turmoil in Terraflippia, and no solution has been found. Even the magic of the grand wizard hasn't helped.

The grand wizard, realizing the impending doom of Terraflippia, has recognized that the only way to restore balance and order between the two factions is to generate magic from a parallel world - from the human world. But how? Humans have so much creativity, but how can it be consolidated and converted to magic?

He then remembered the great power that color inherently generates and devised a color magic spell. The wizard added the idea to an artist's thoughts prompting him to create a coloring book that represents the two factions in 25 magical flip illustrations.

The spell was placed on imagery that balances the two factions, and restores magic to Terraflippia.

To the artist the coloring book and this story are just a part of his imagination, but to Terraflippia they are much more. The two factions on each page represent different sides of the same coin, and a balance between the two.

The magic happens when humans around the globe access their creativity to give these illustrations the life of color. Now the magic is up to you. The views you see and the color you give to them have the capacity to save Terraflippia and bring peace.

The grand wizard asks all colorists to color what is in their hearts, but also to remember that appearances aren't everything. What is ugly on the outside isn't always ugly on the inside.

The fate of Terraflippia is in your hands!

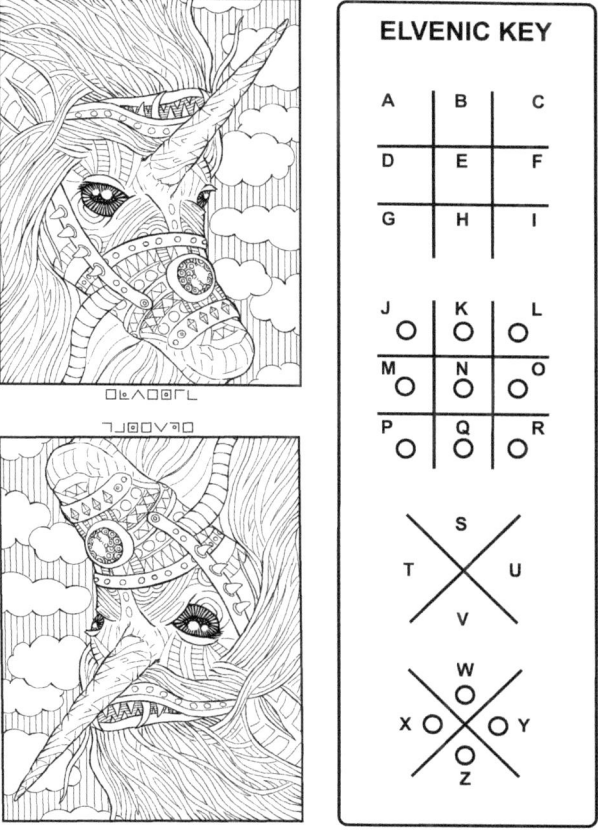

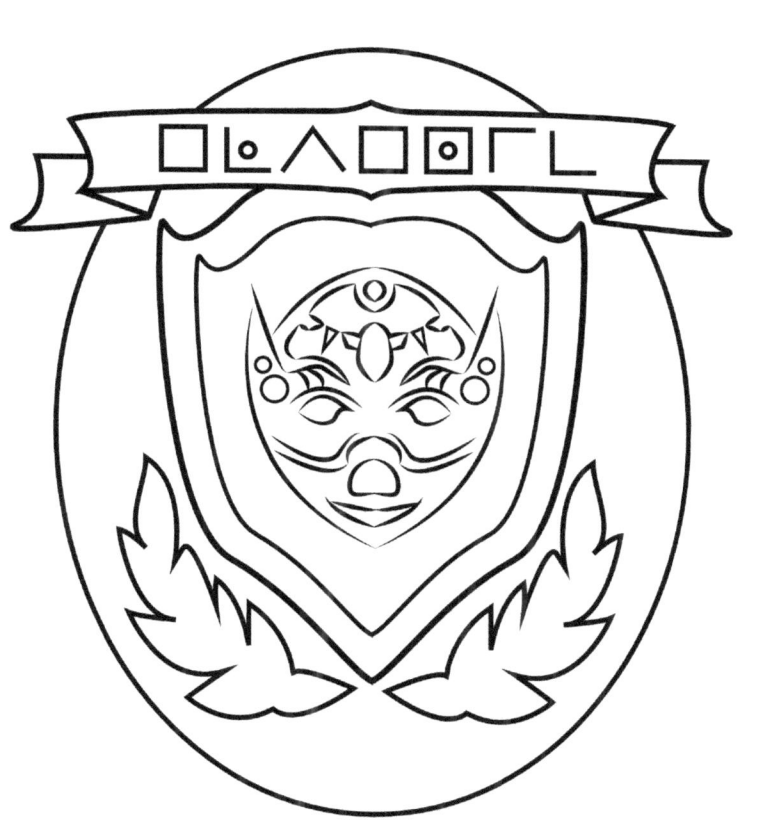

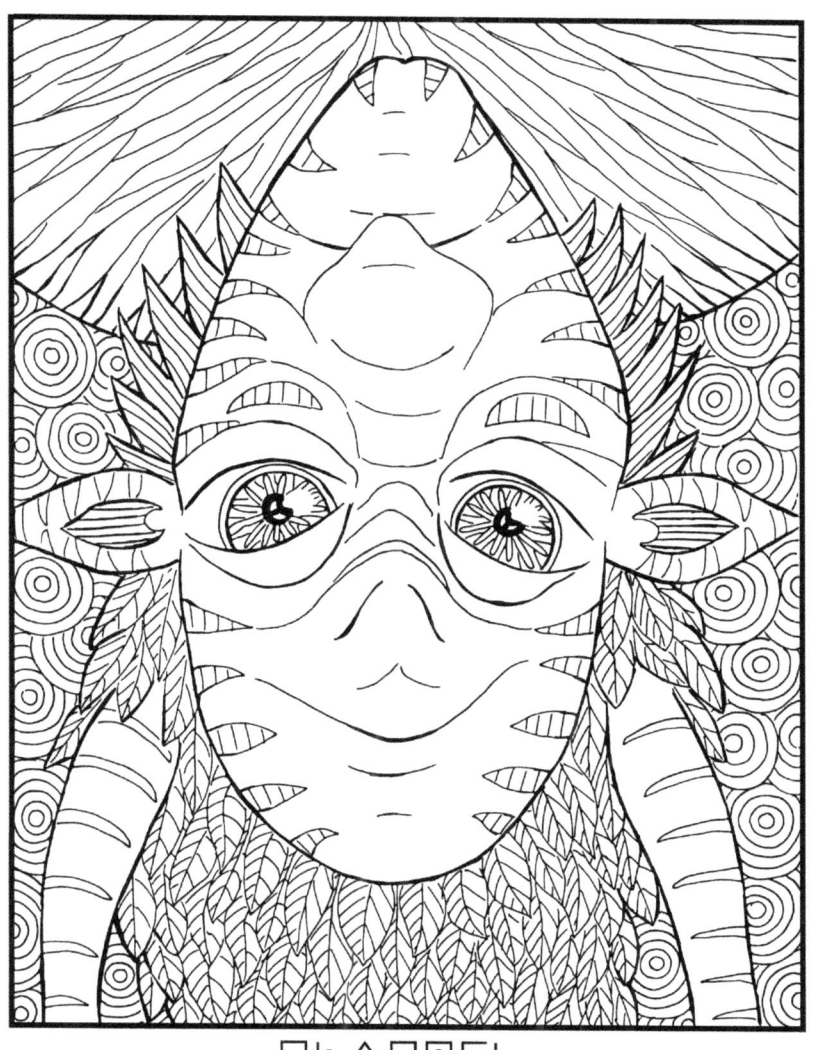

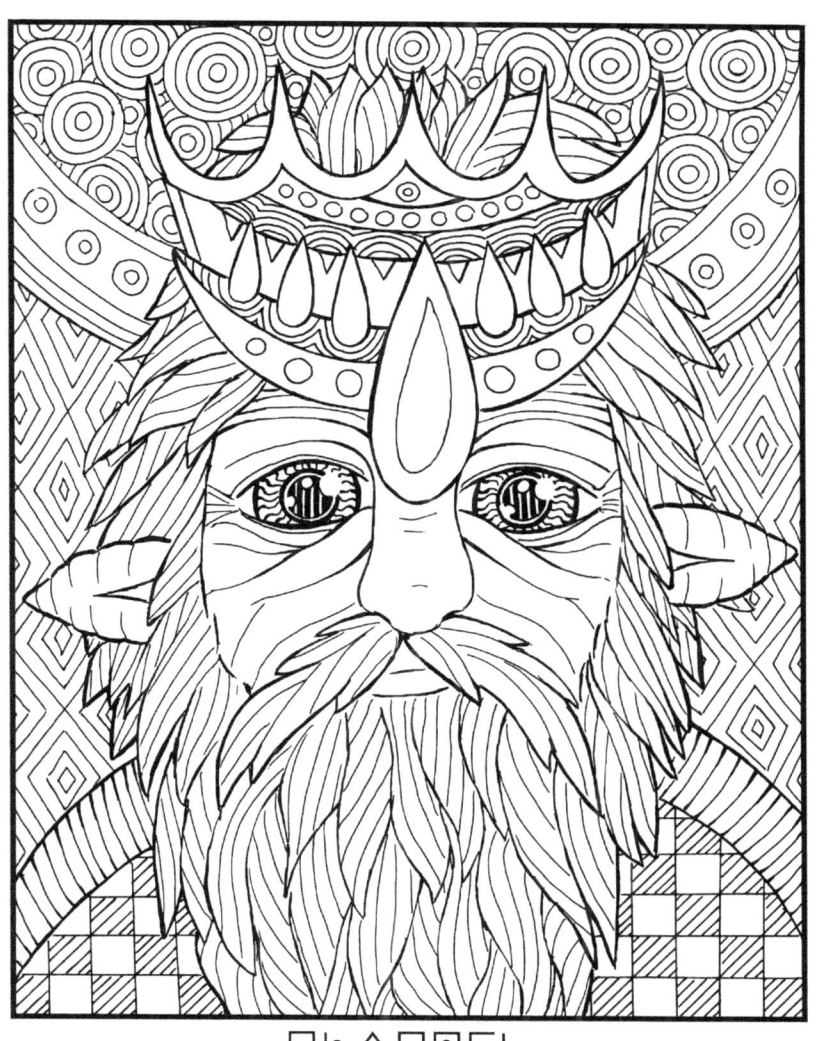

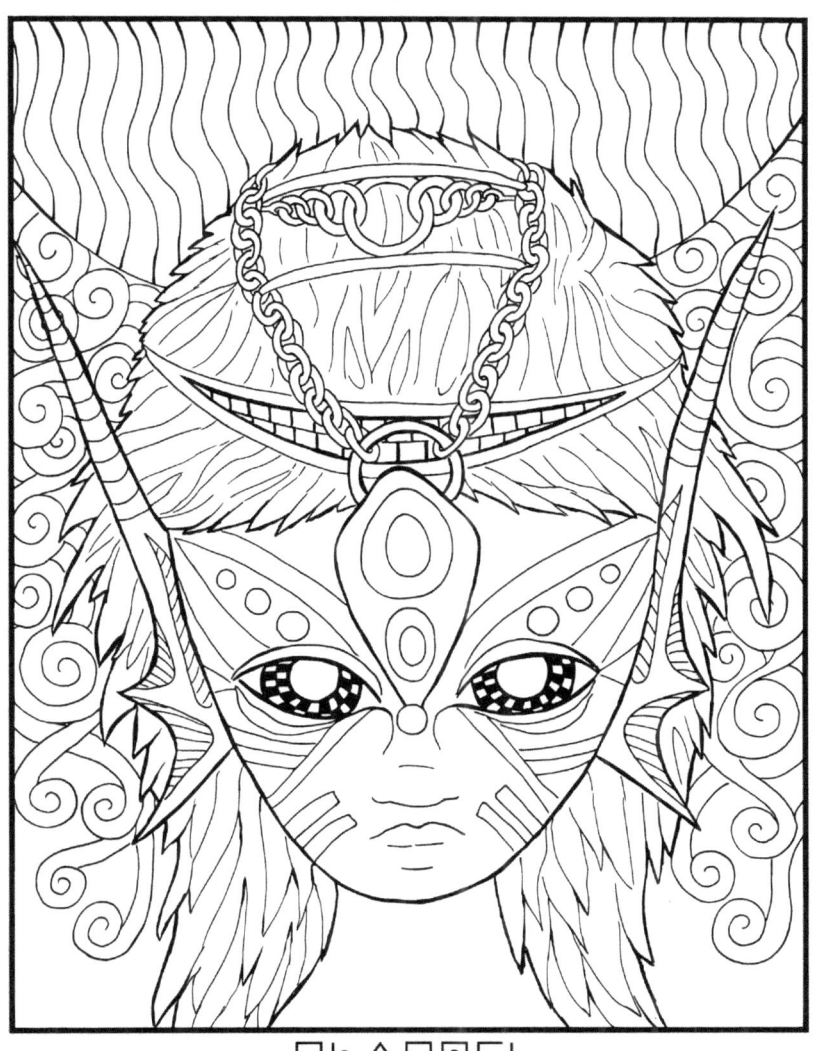

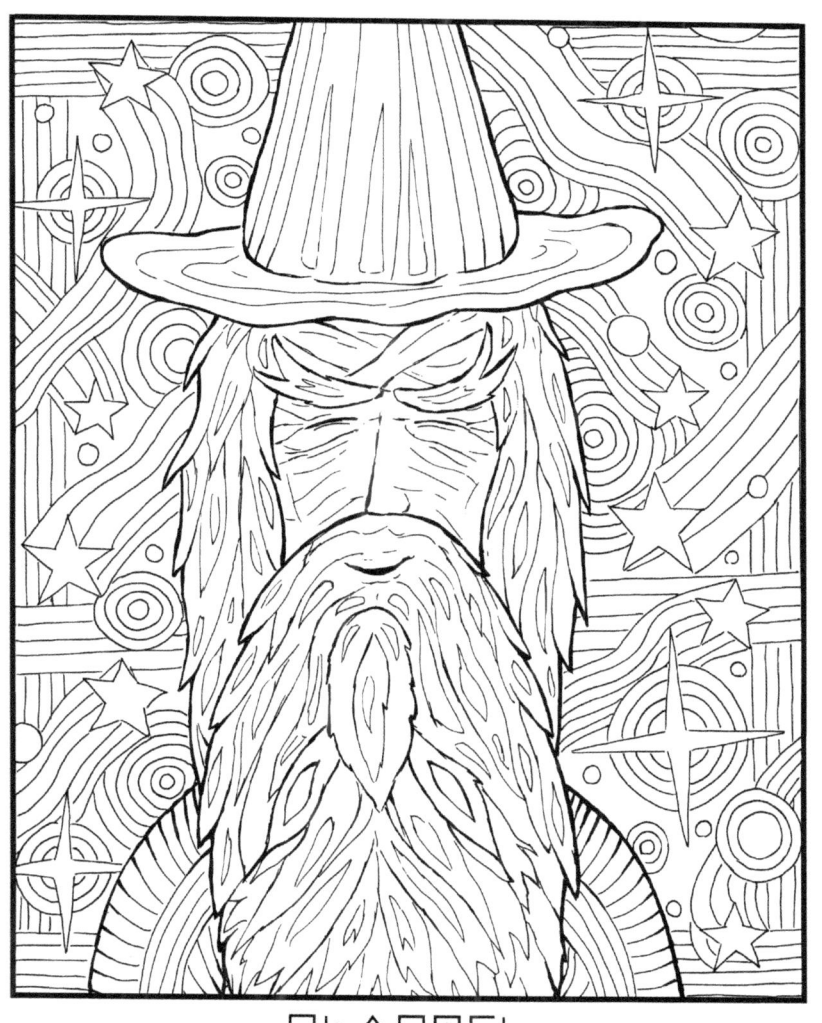

WIZARD

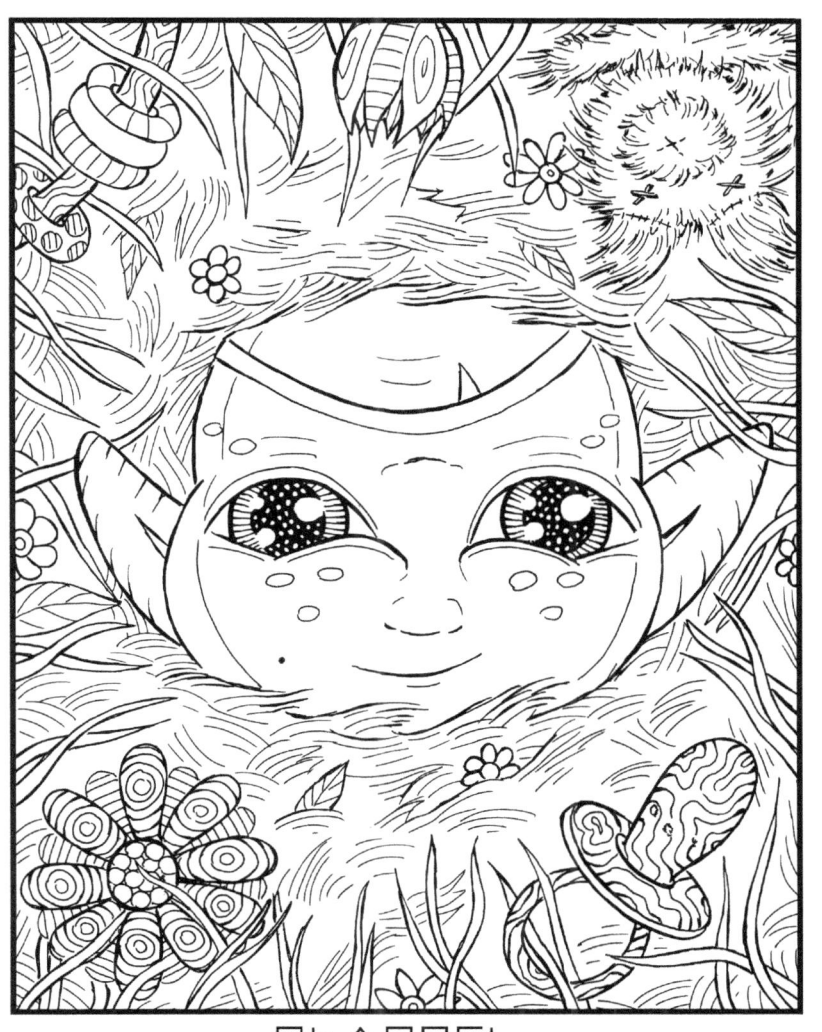

□□ᒪᐱ◻◻ᒥᒪ

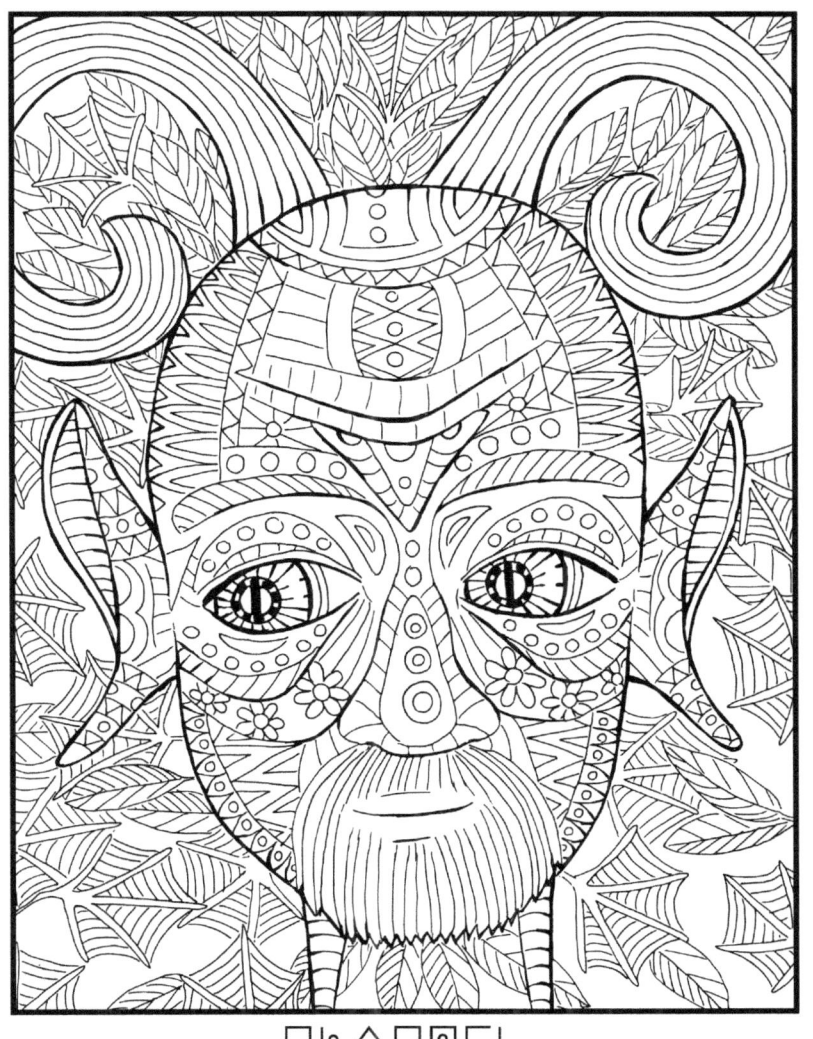

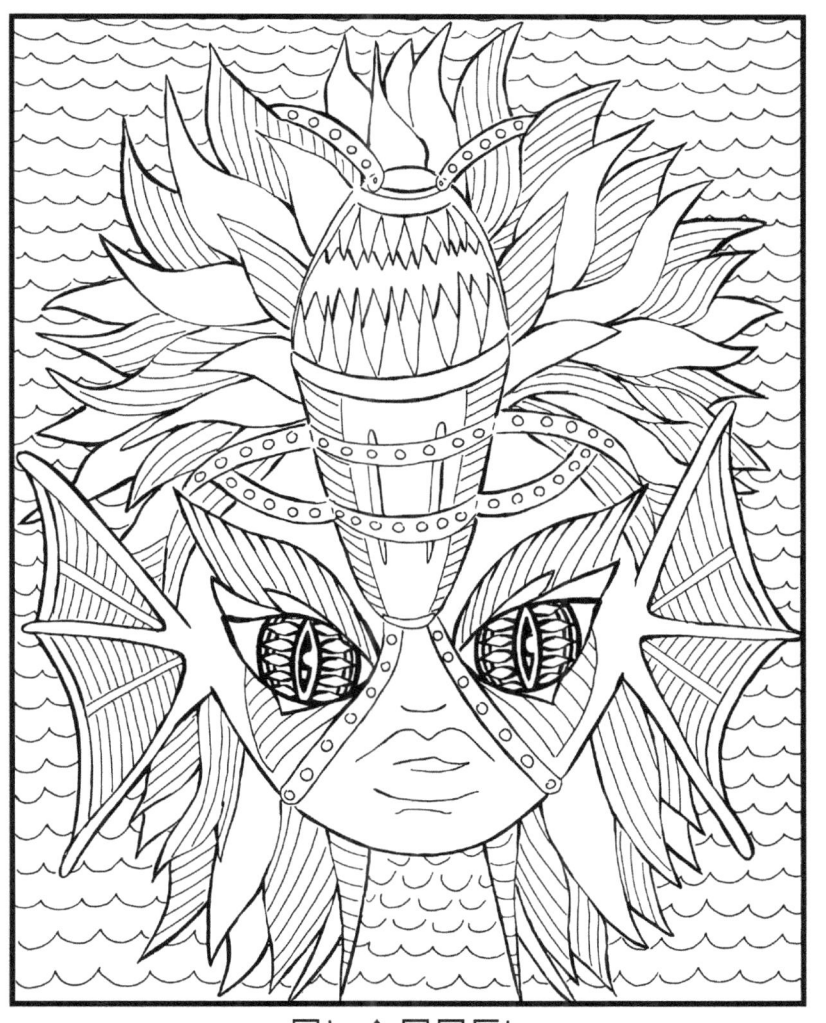

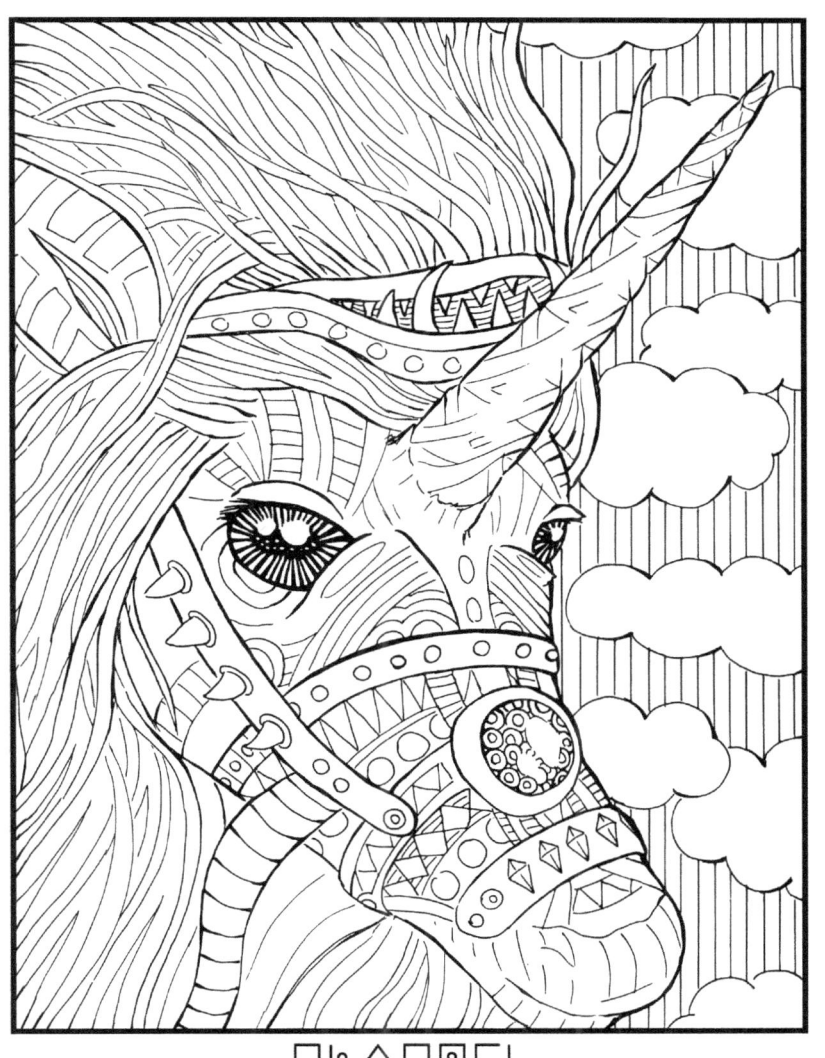

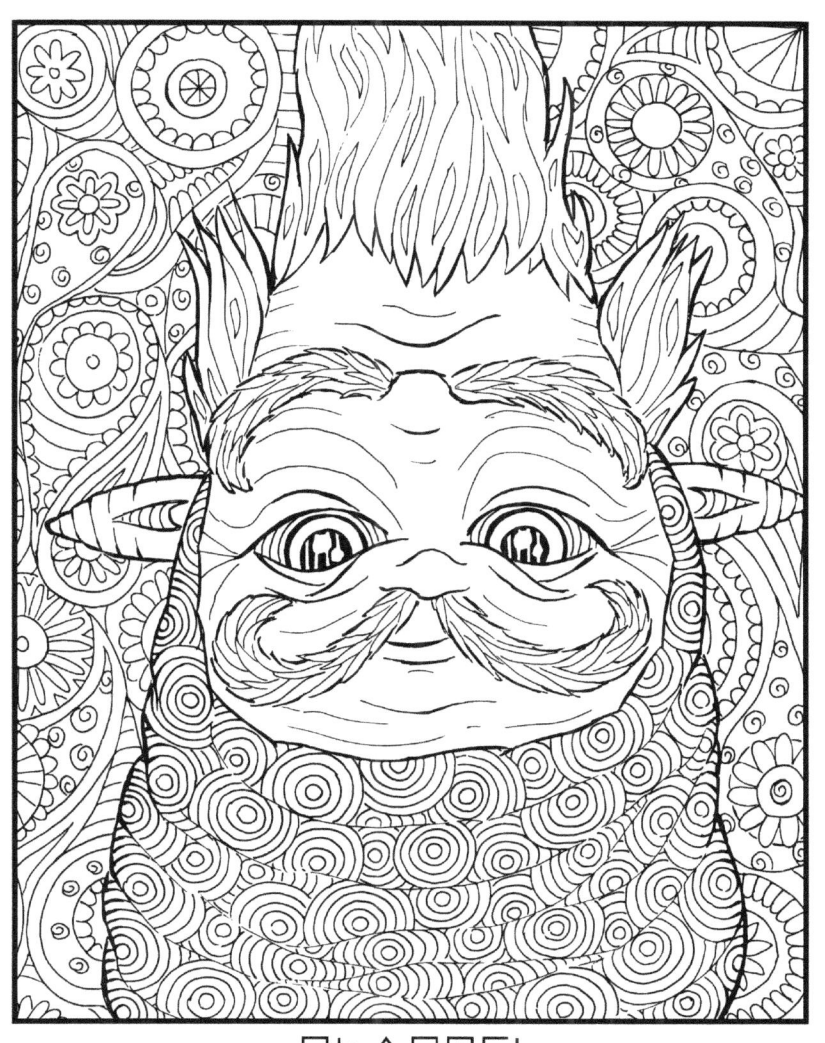

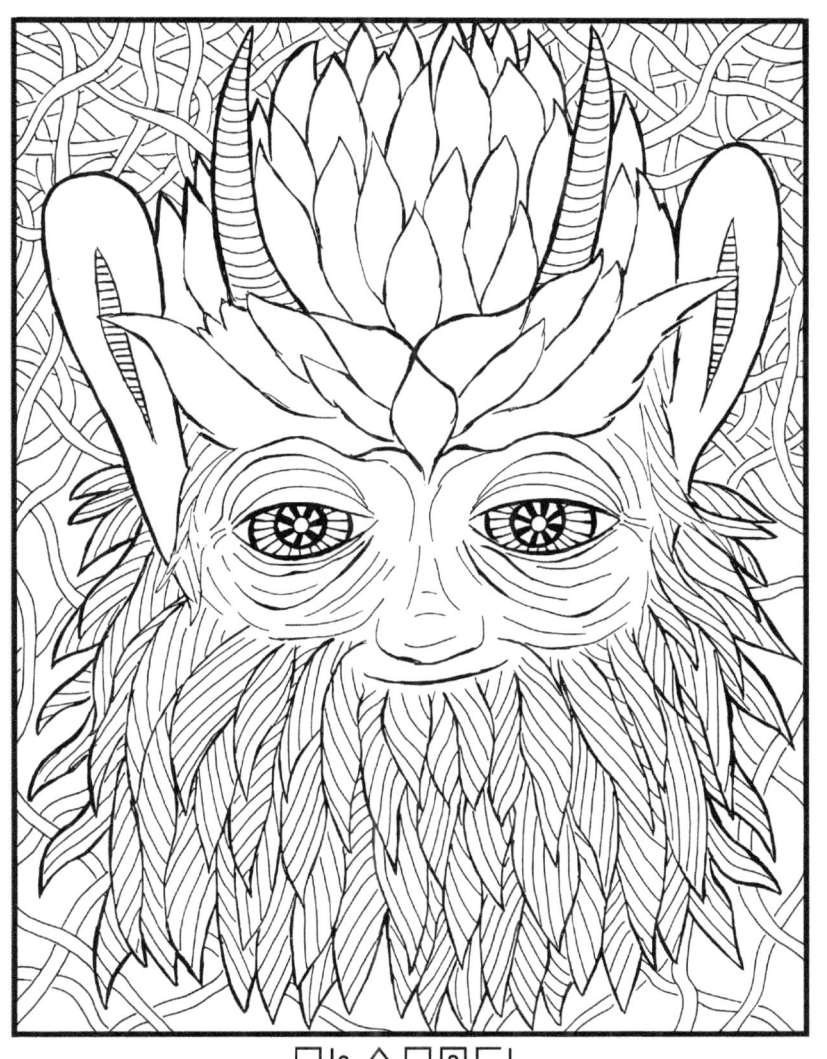

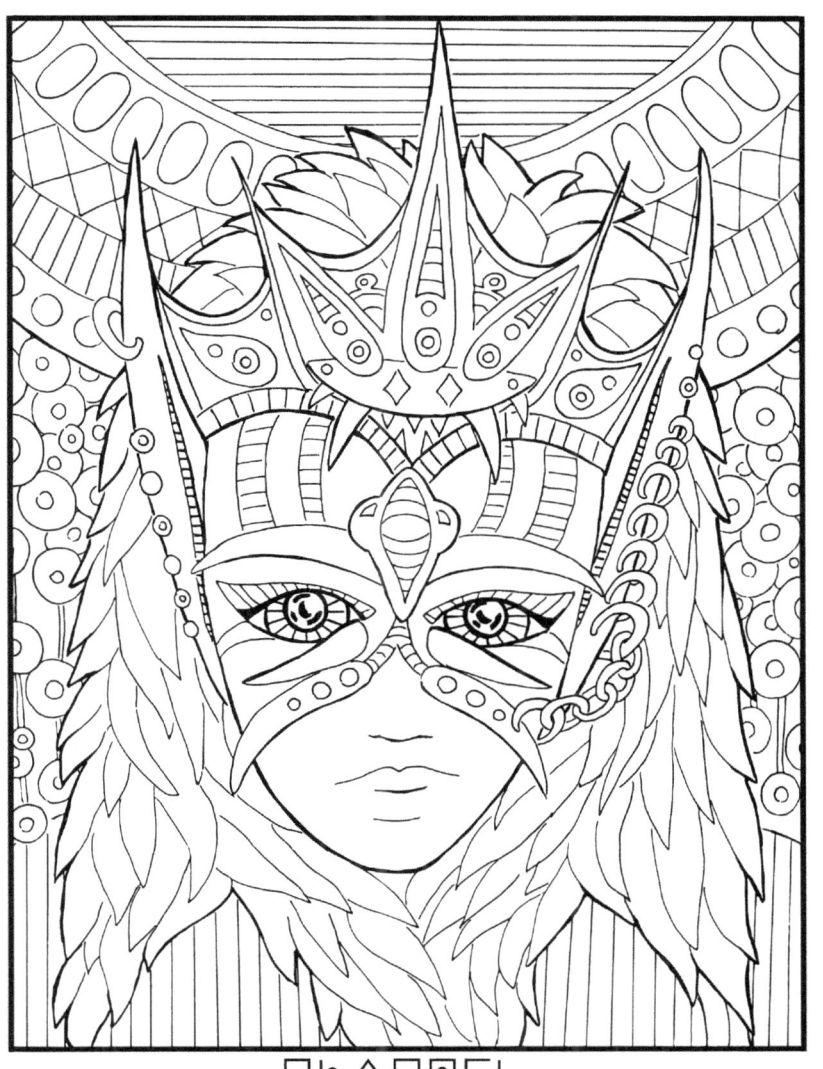

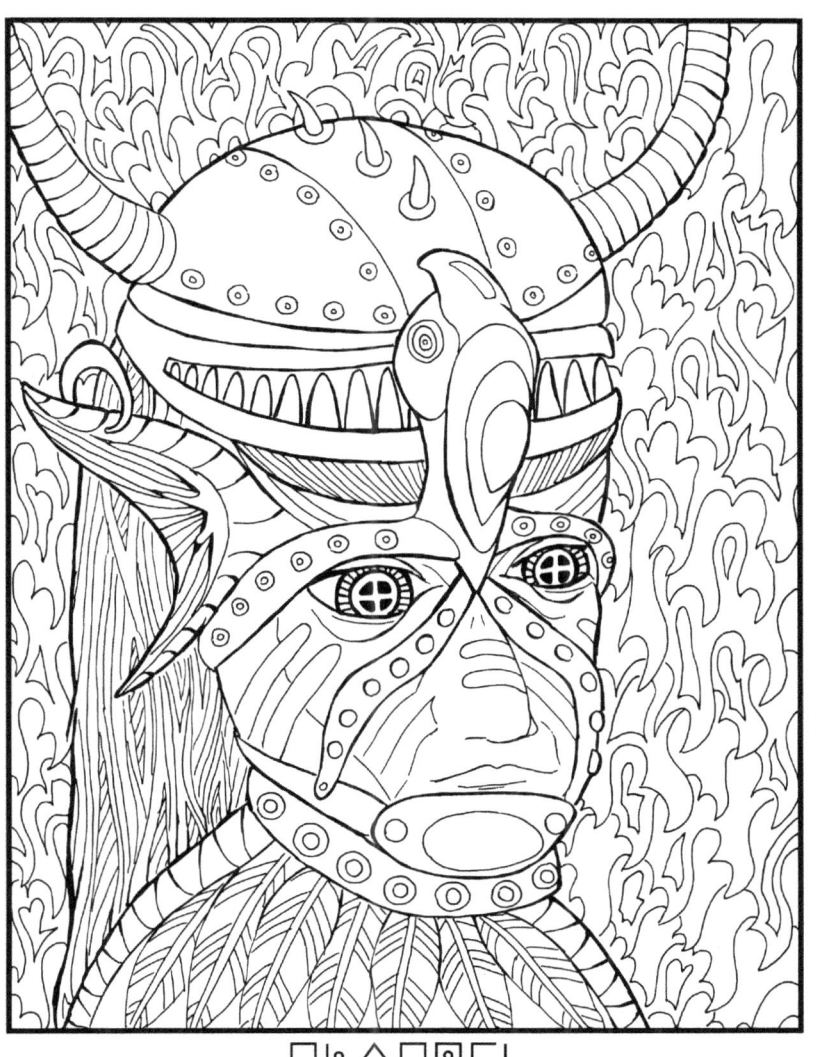

ᐅᓕᐊᑐᒡᒪ

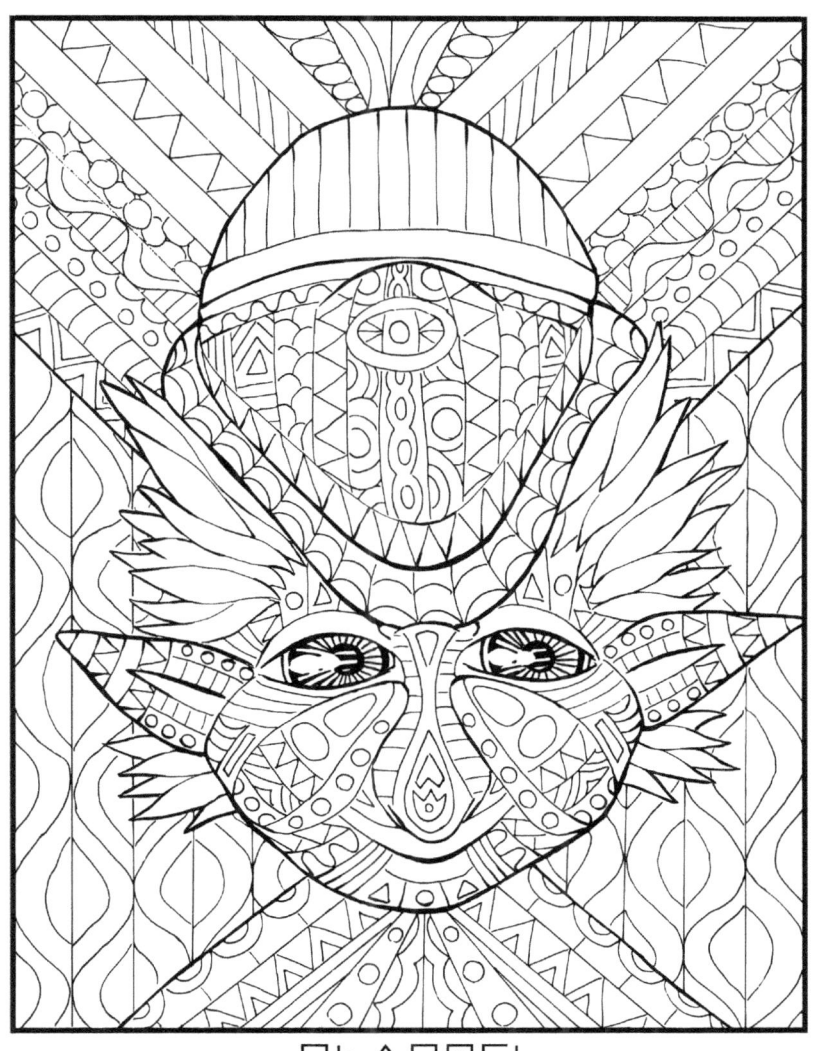

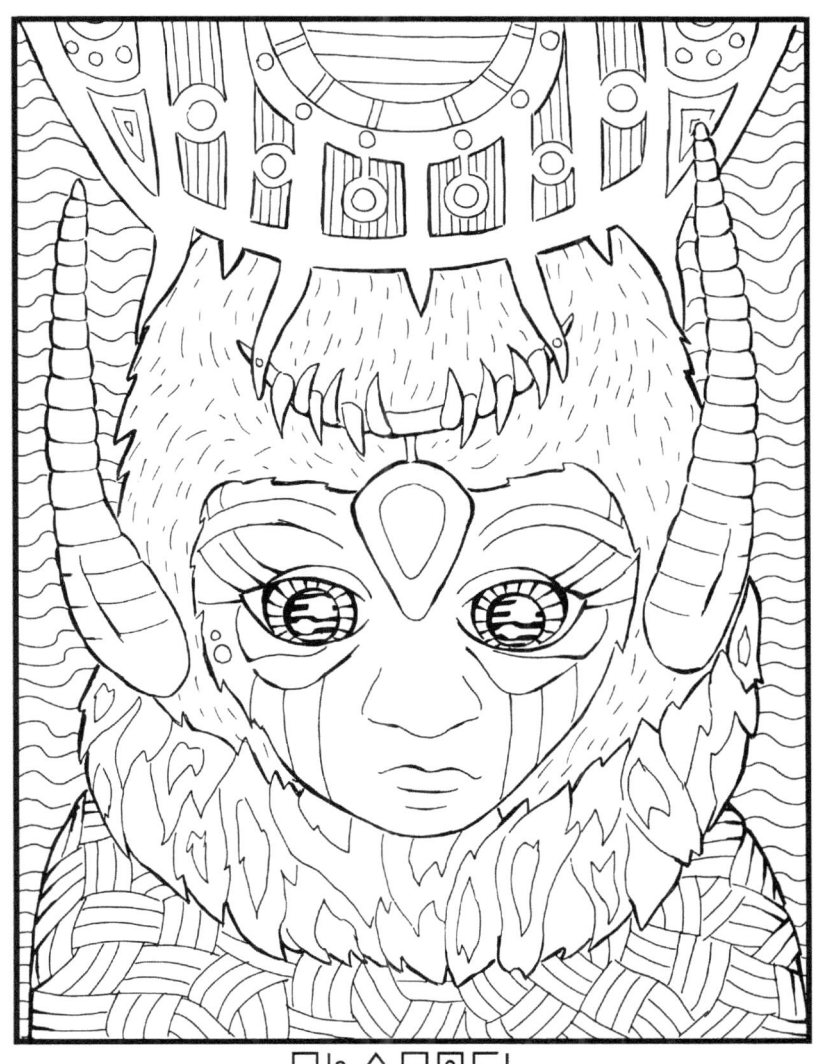

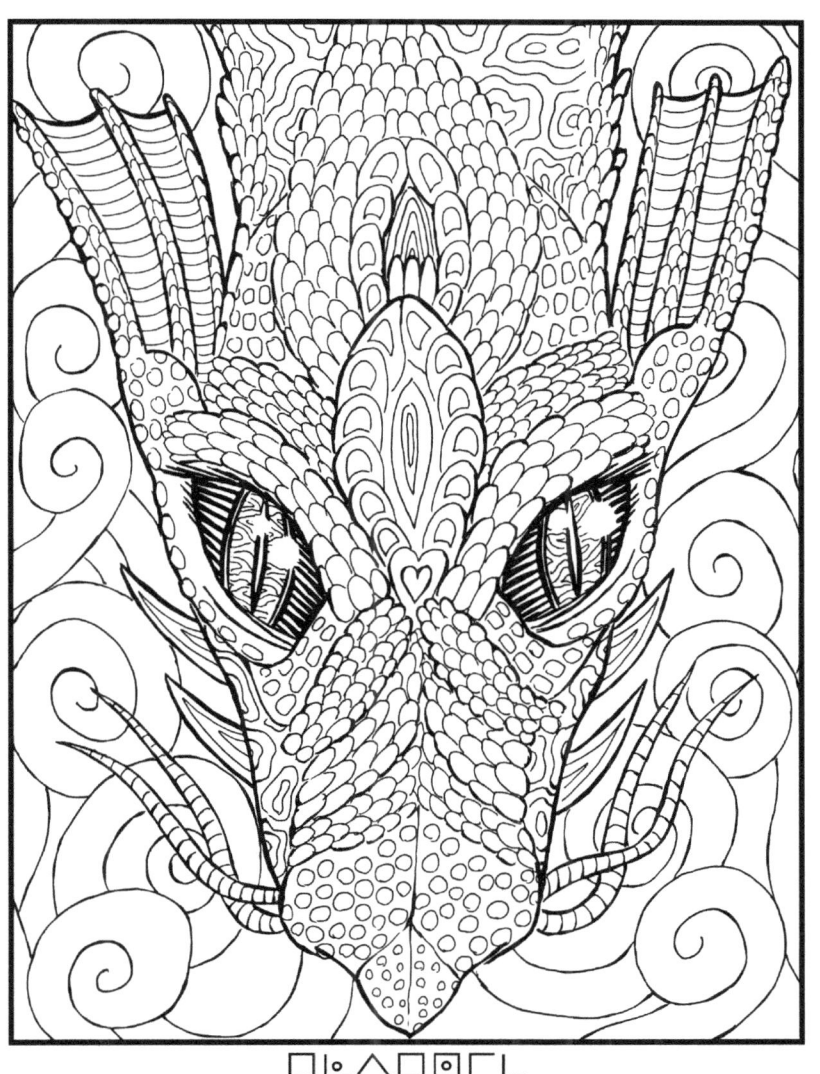

□ㄴ∧□□ㄱㄴ

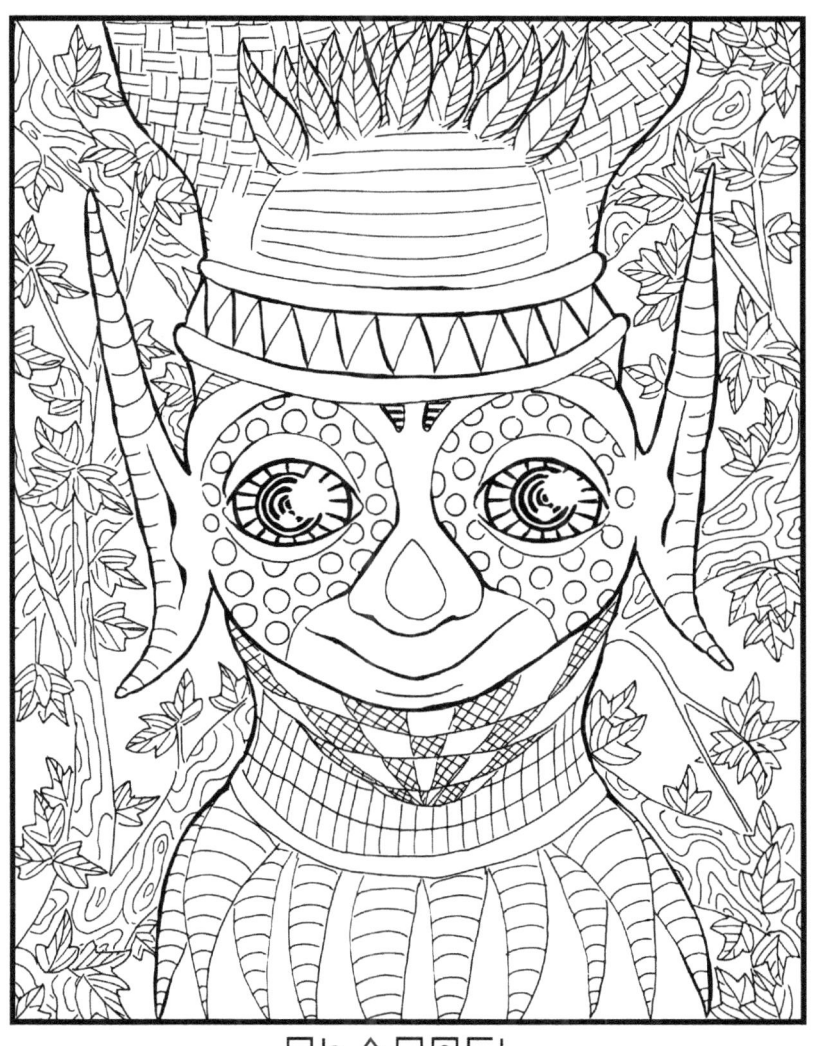

ⵎⵍⴲⴷⵎⵎⵔⵍ

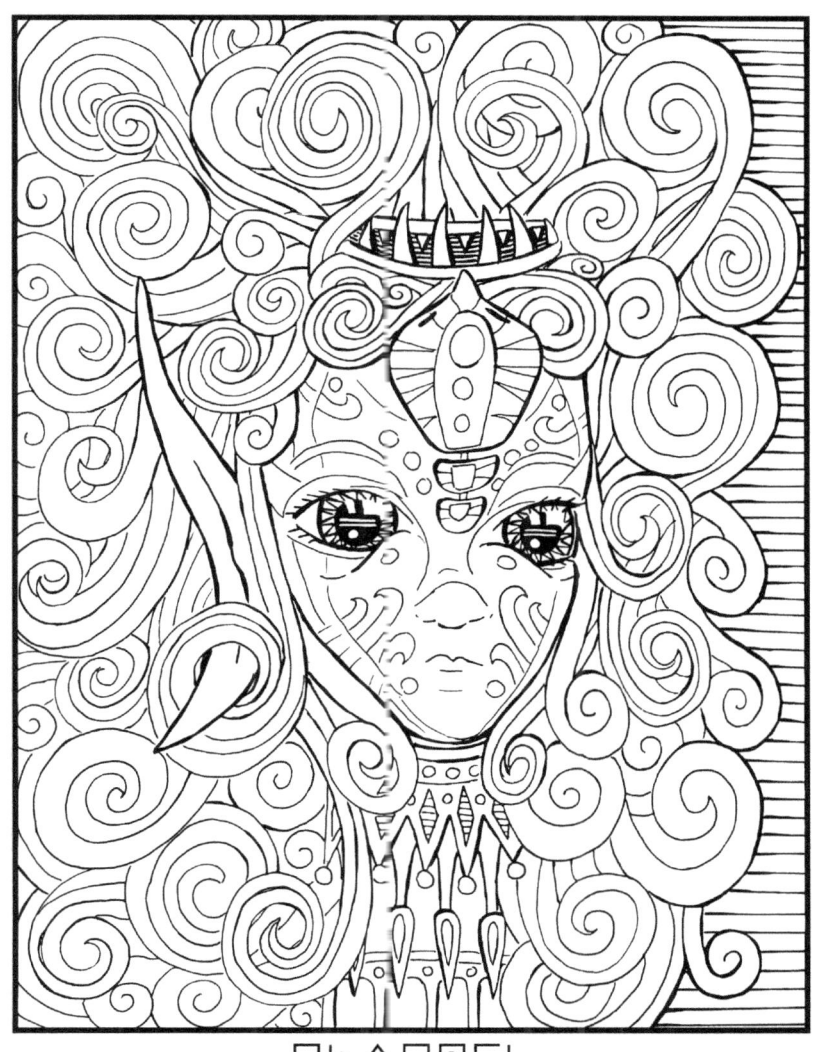

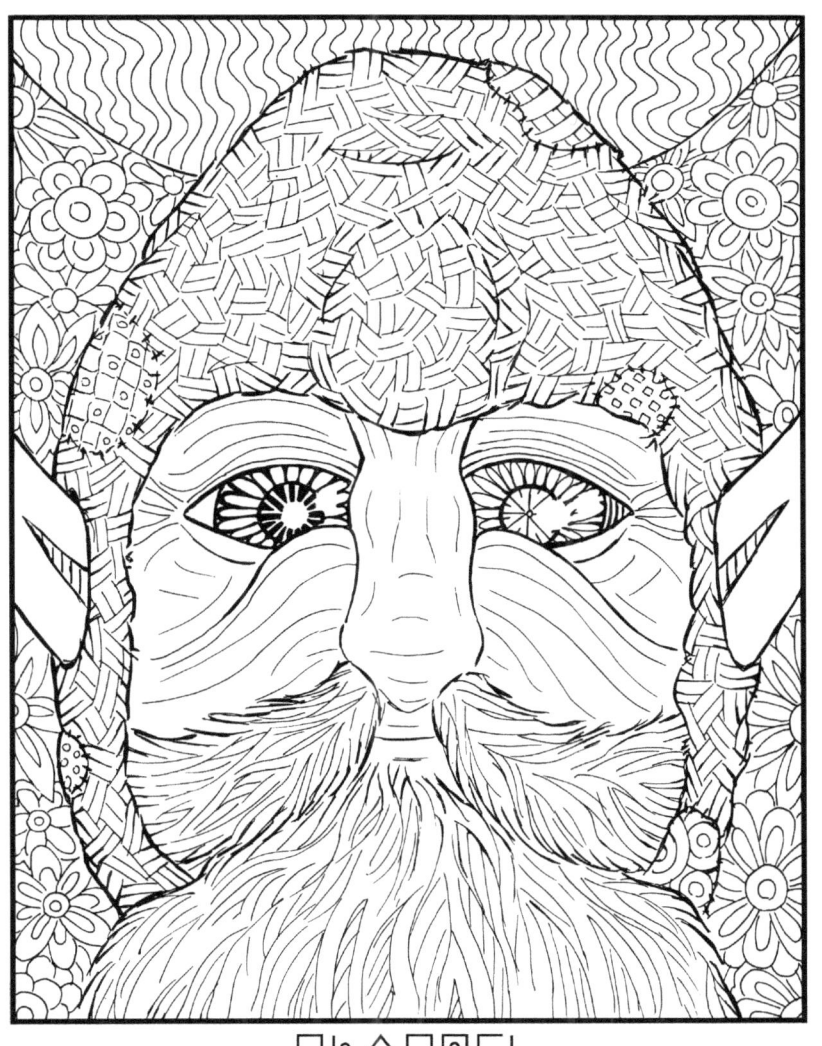

□ᑲ∧▢ʘᒥᒪ

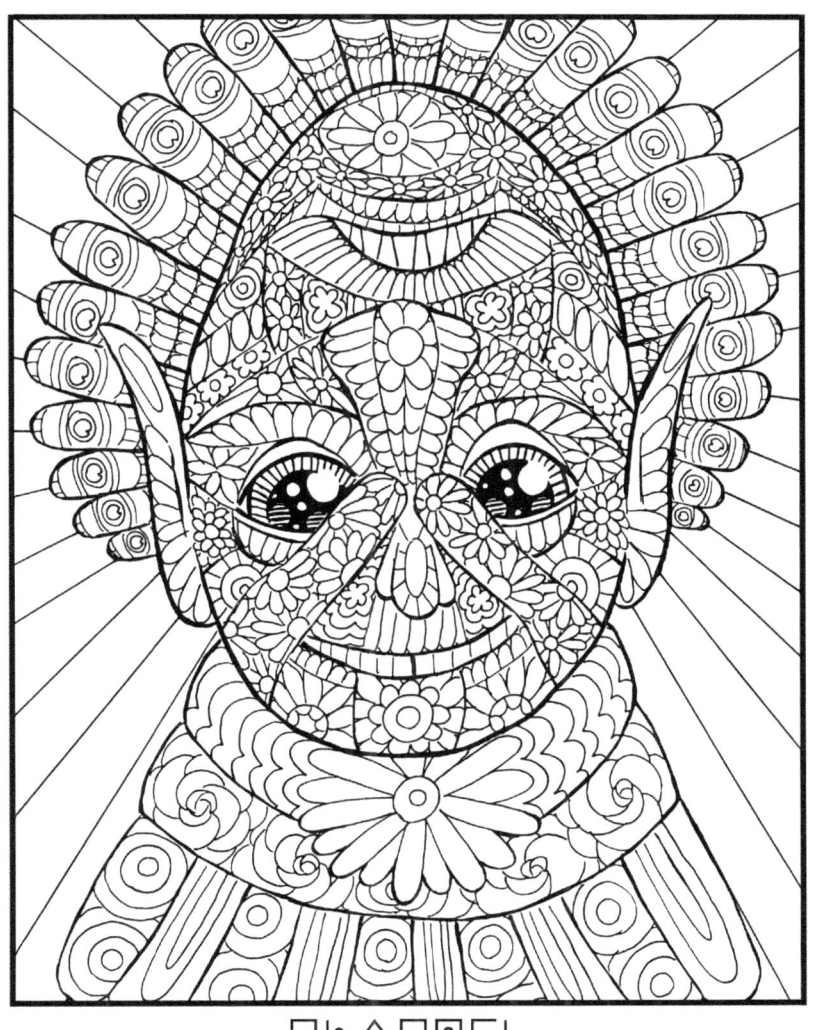

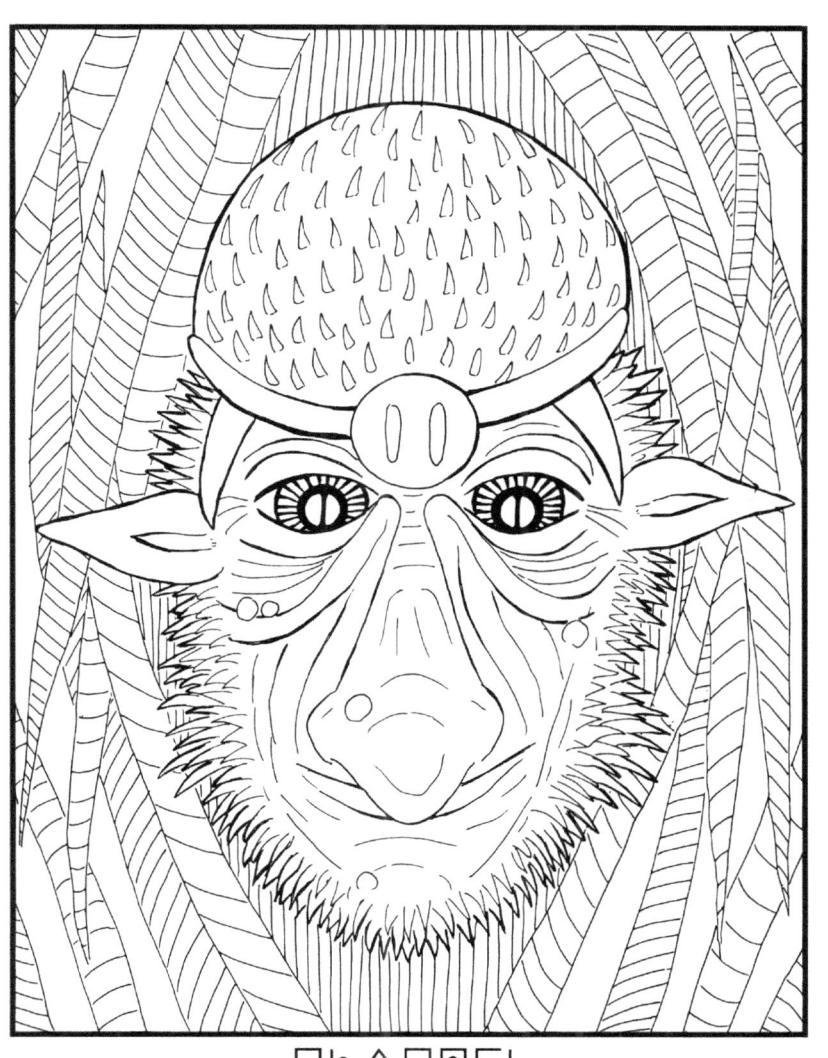

□ʟo∧□ʘᴦʟ

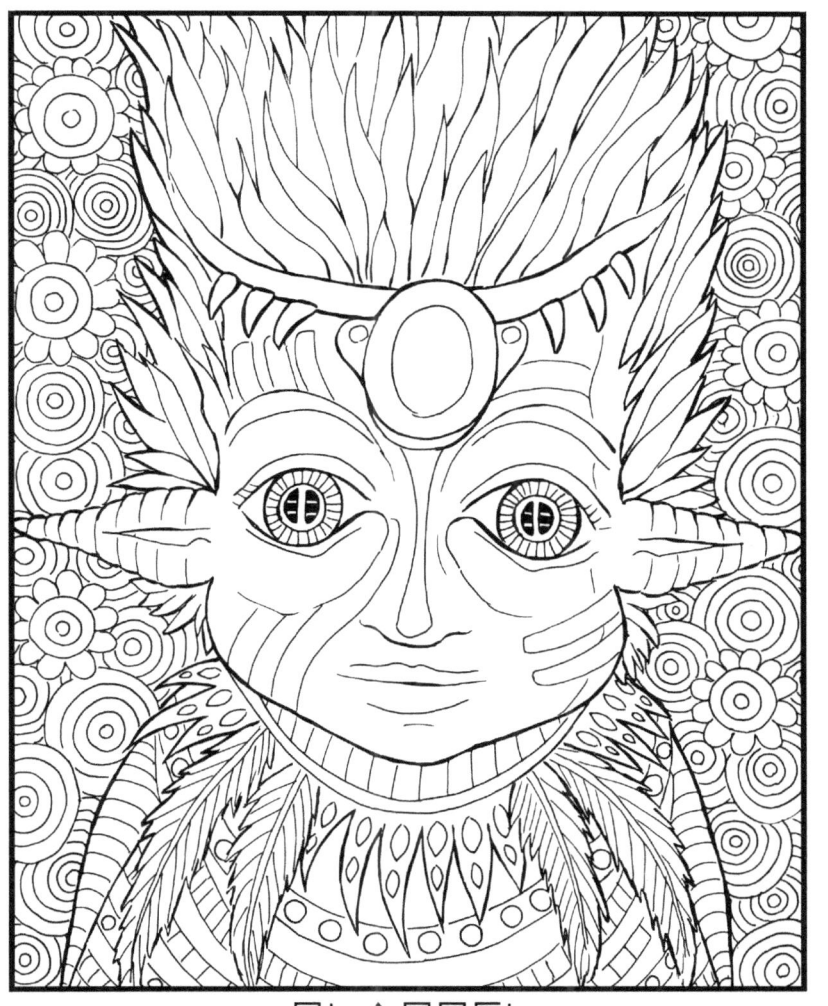

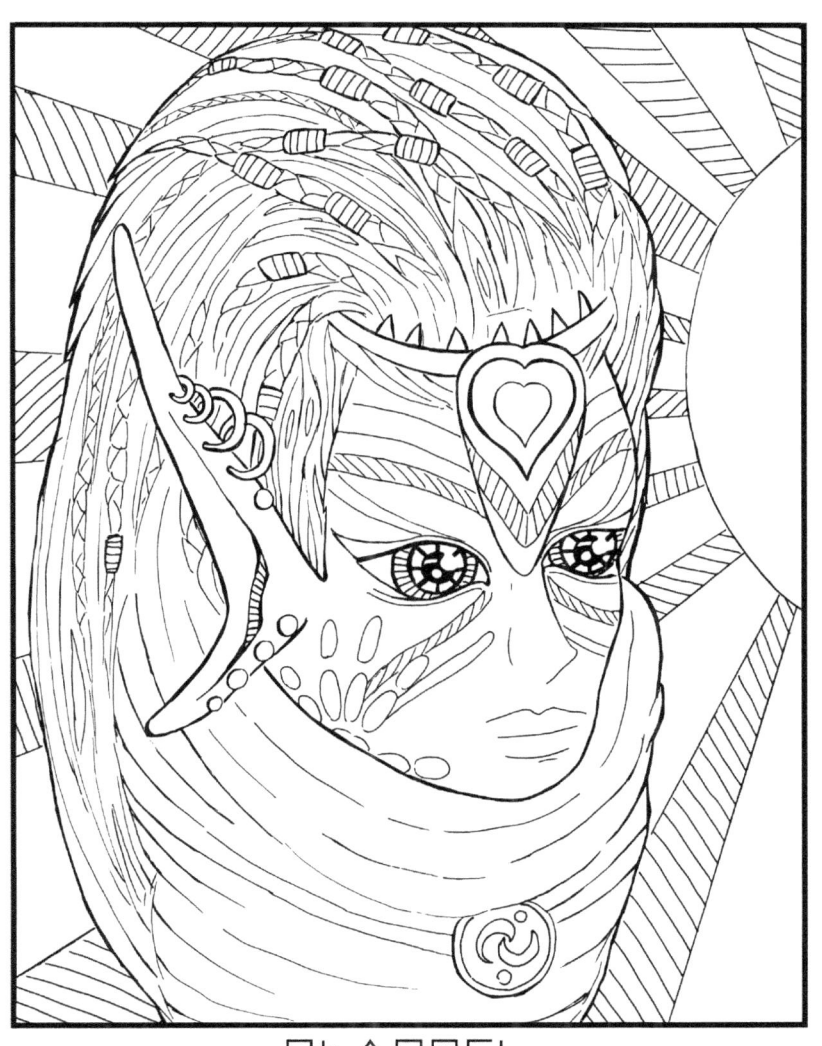

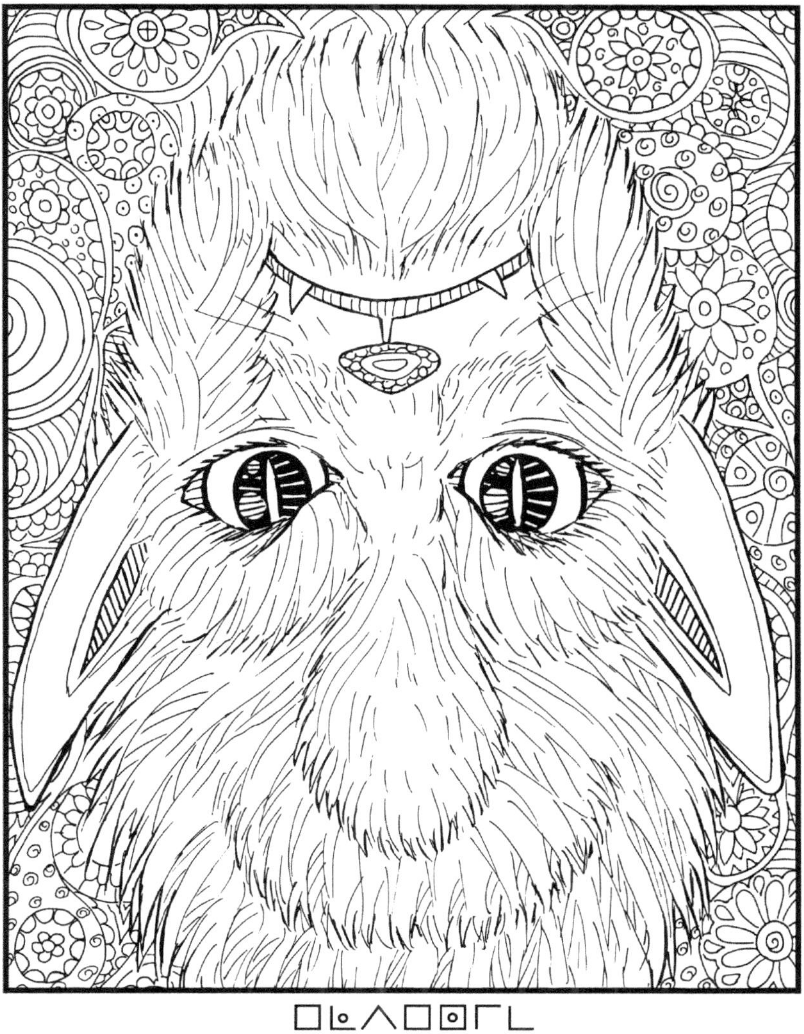

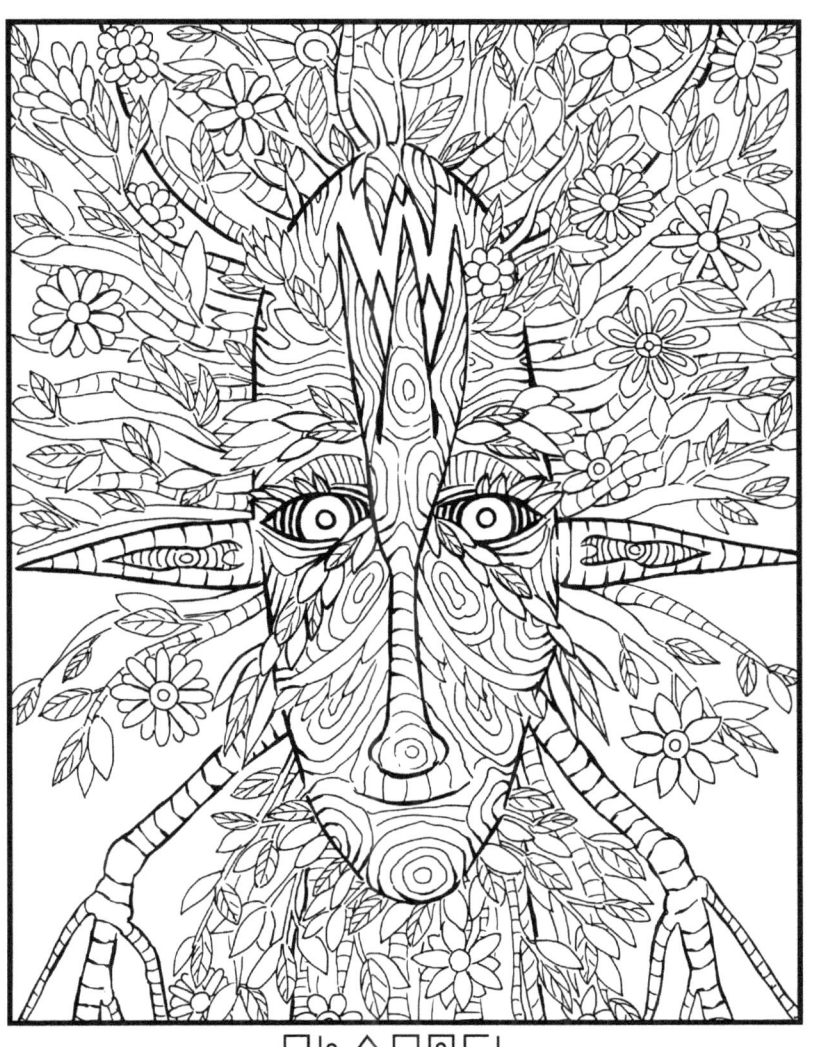

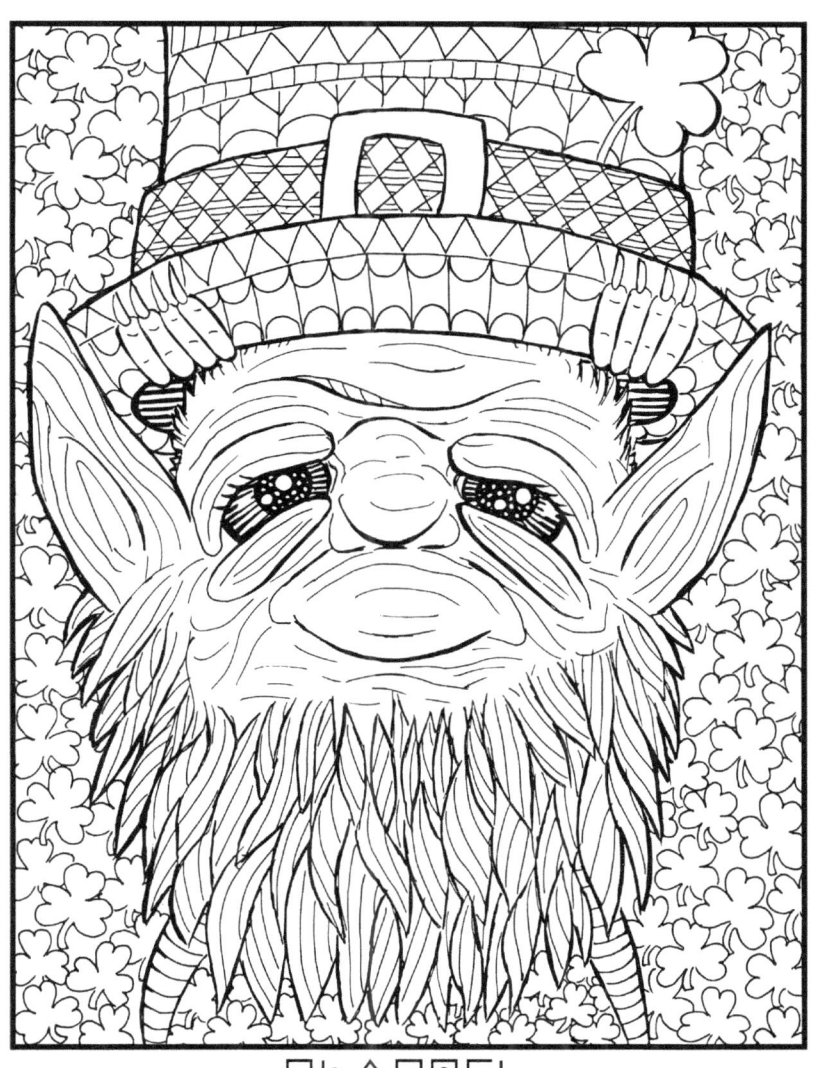

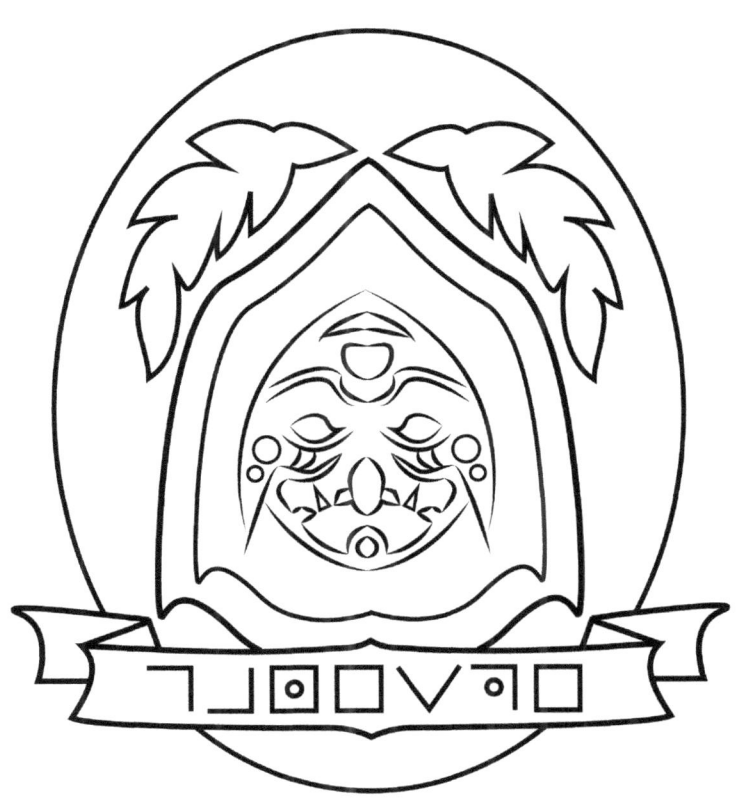

ANOTHER TRY!
(Duplicate Coloring Pages FLIPPED)

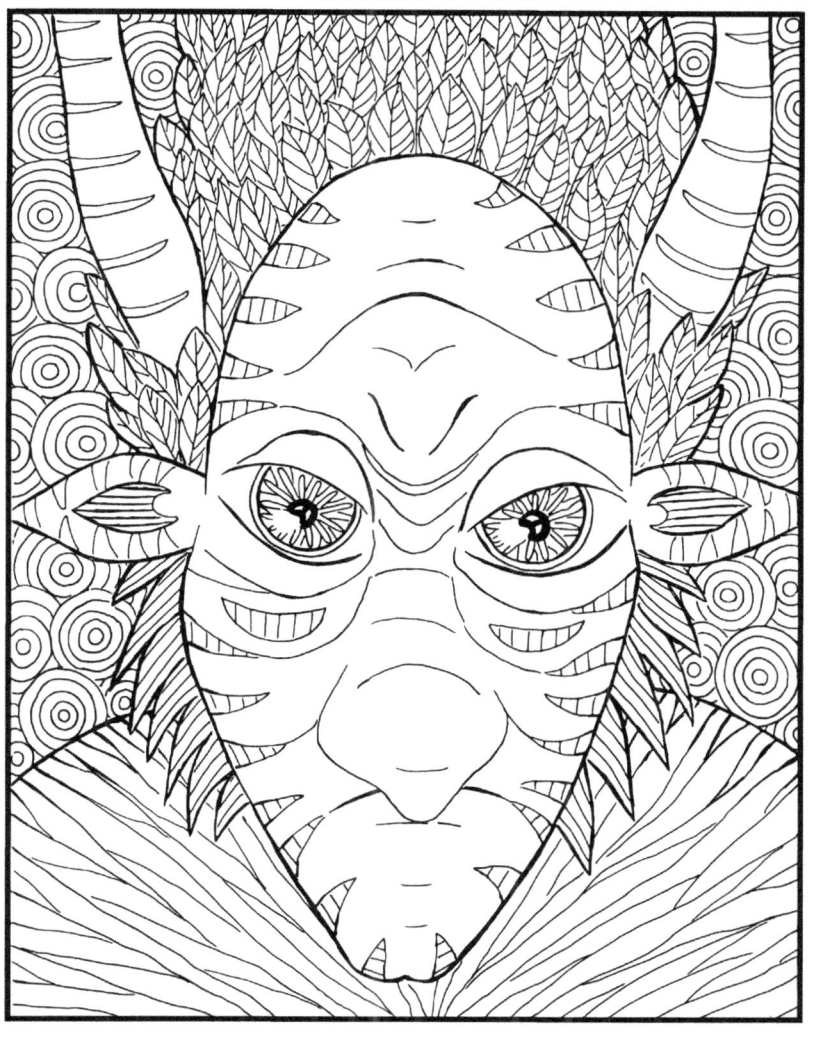

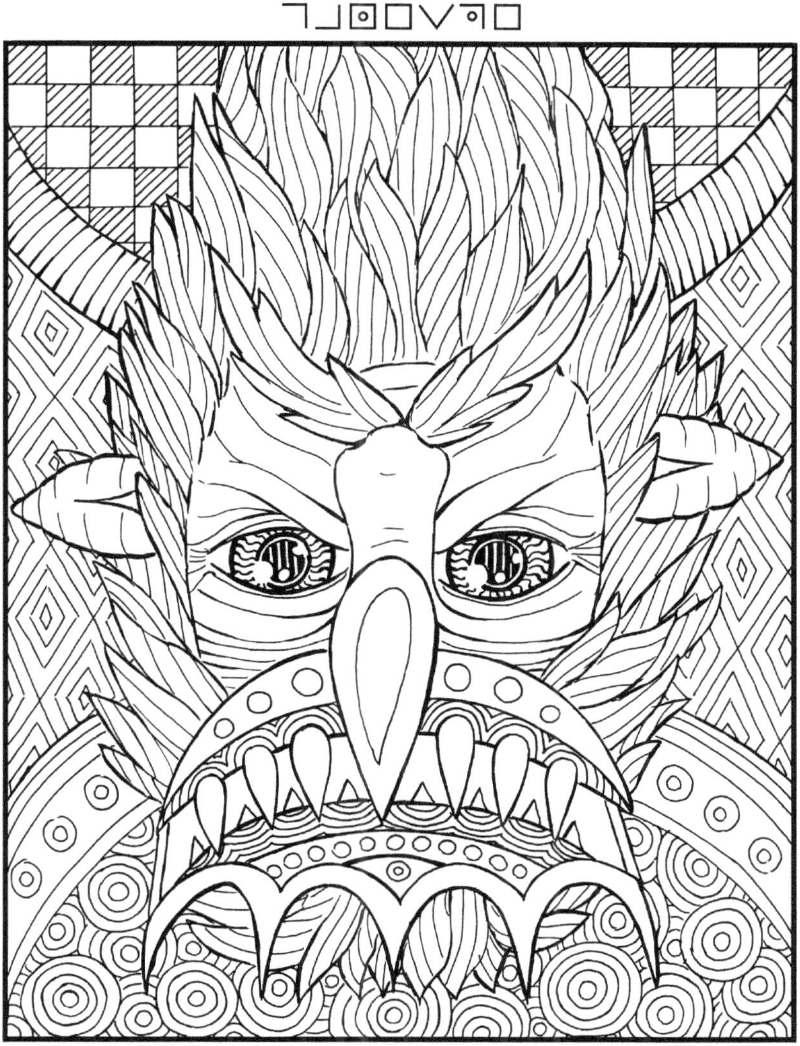

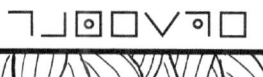

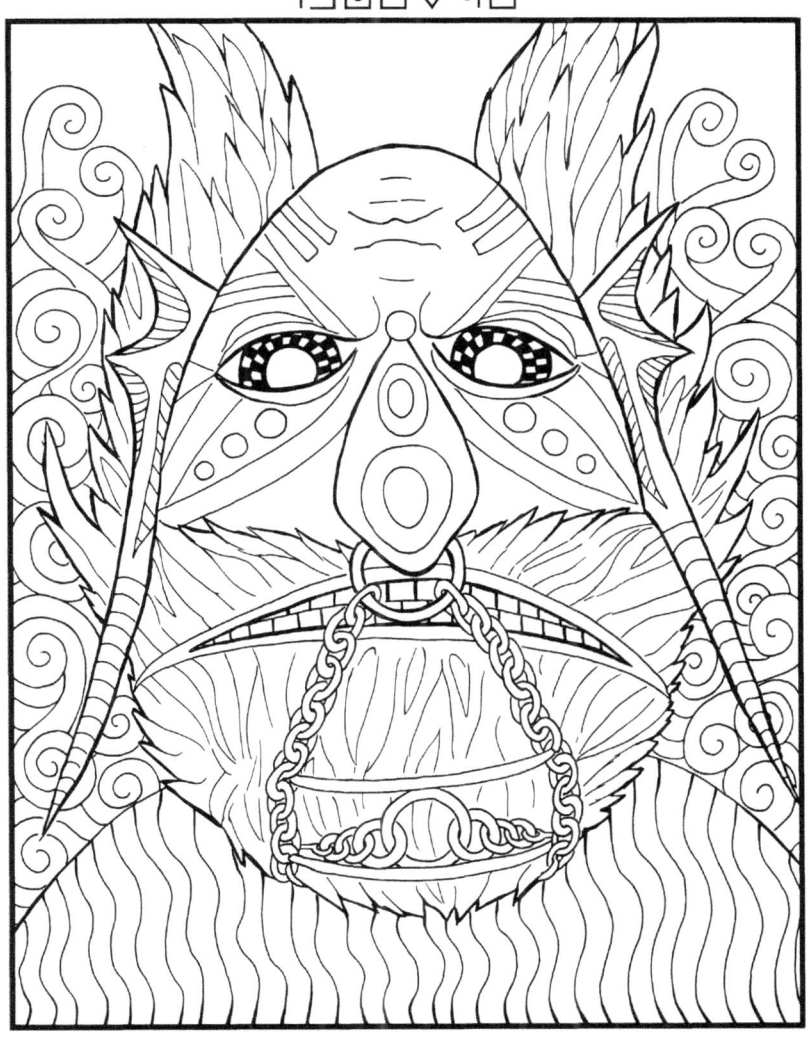

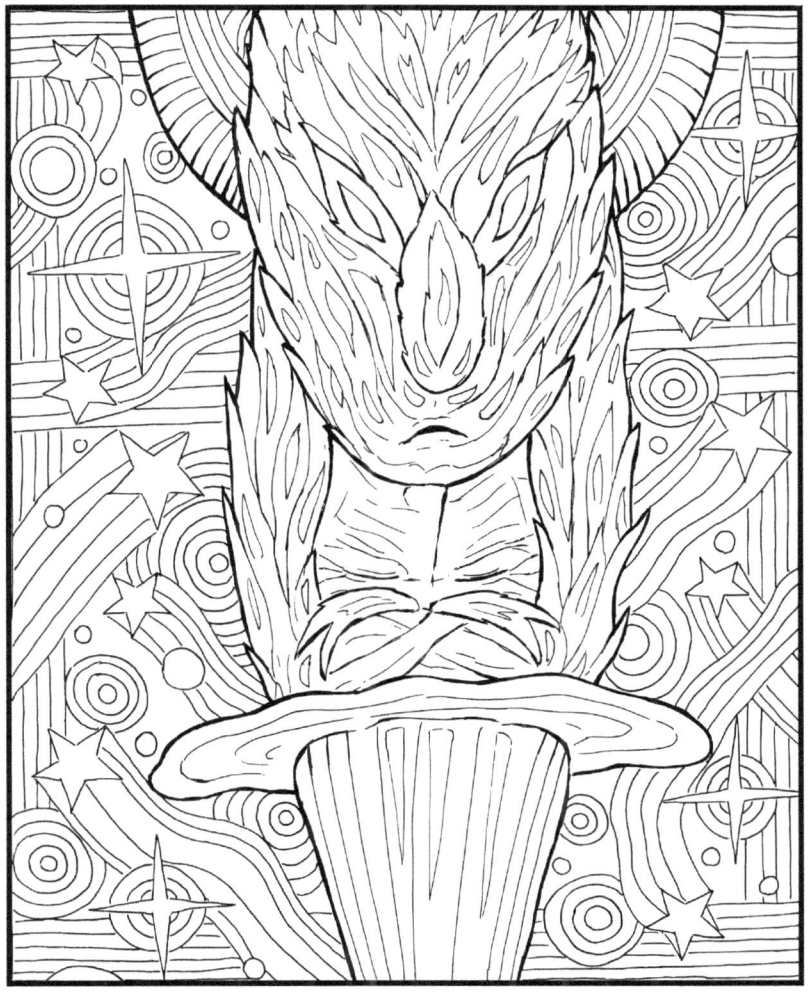

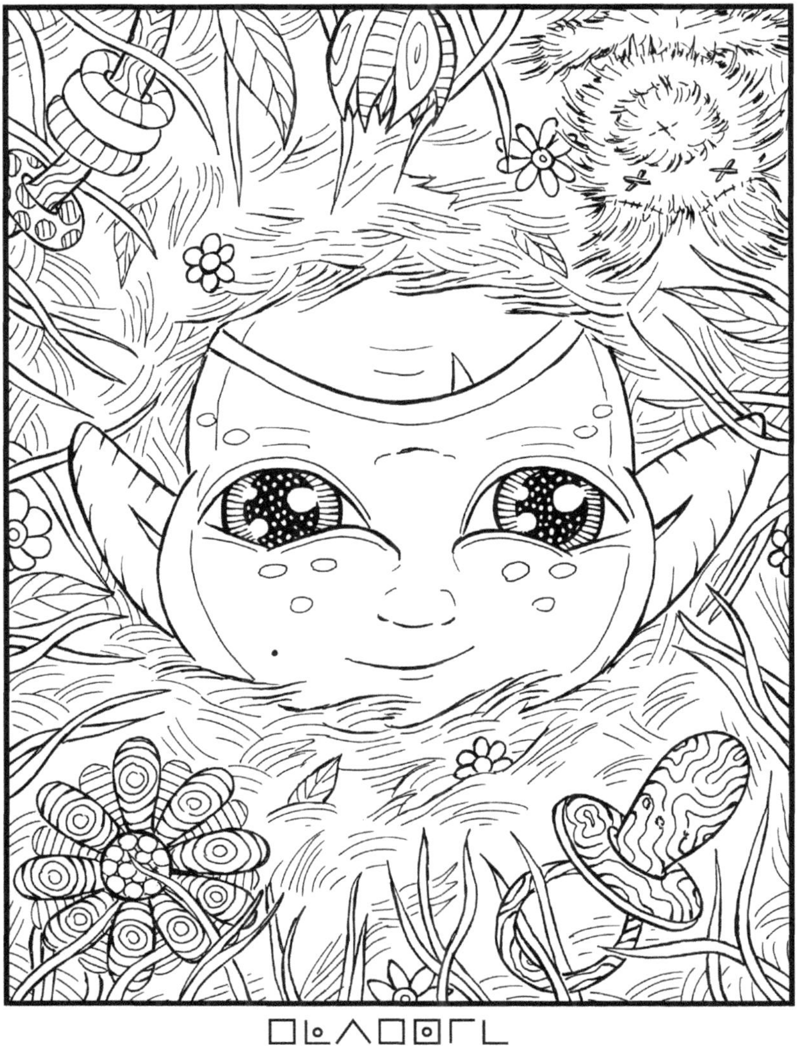

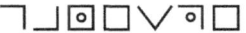

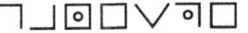

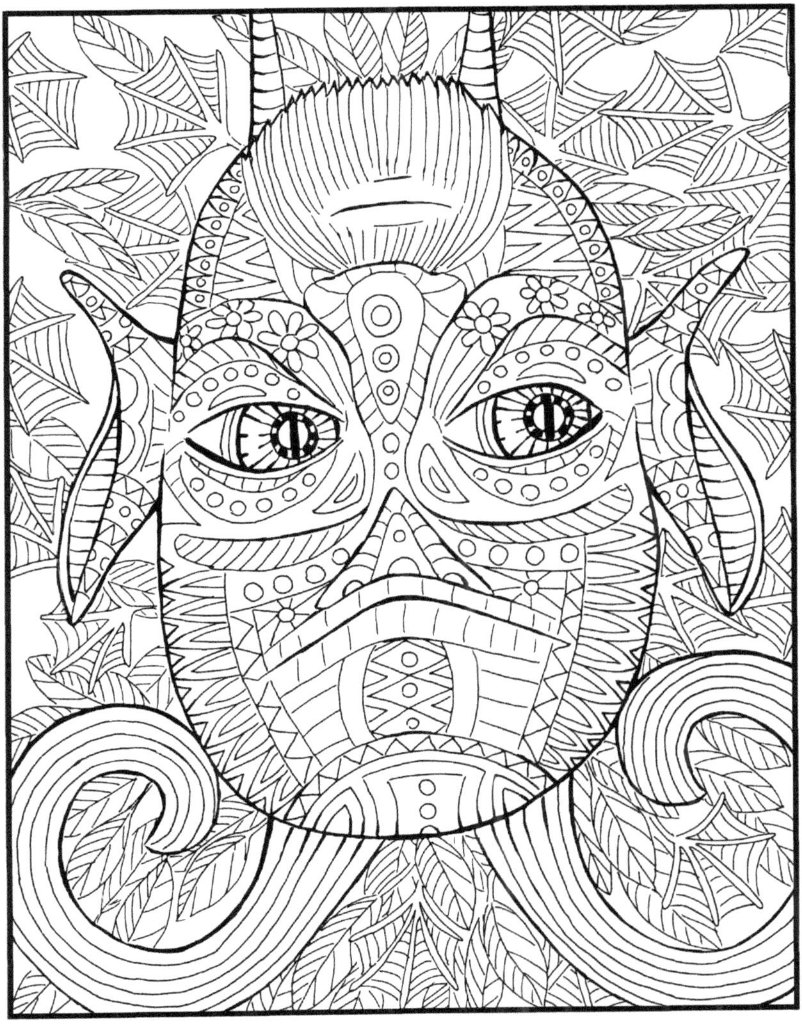

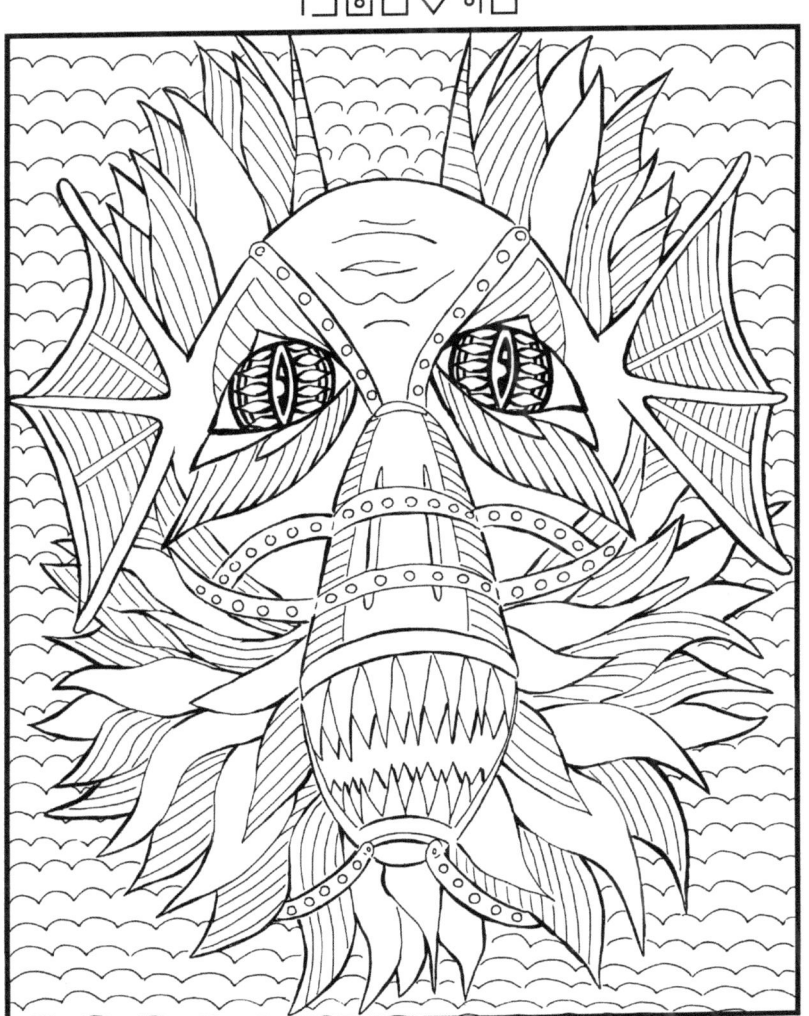

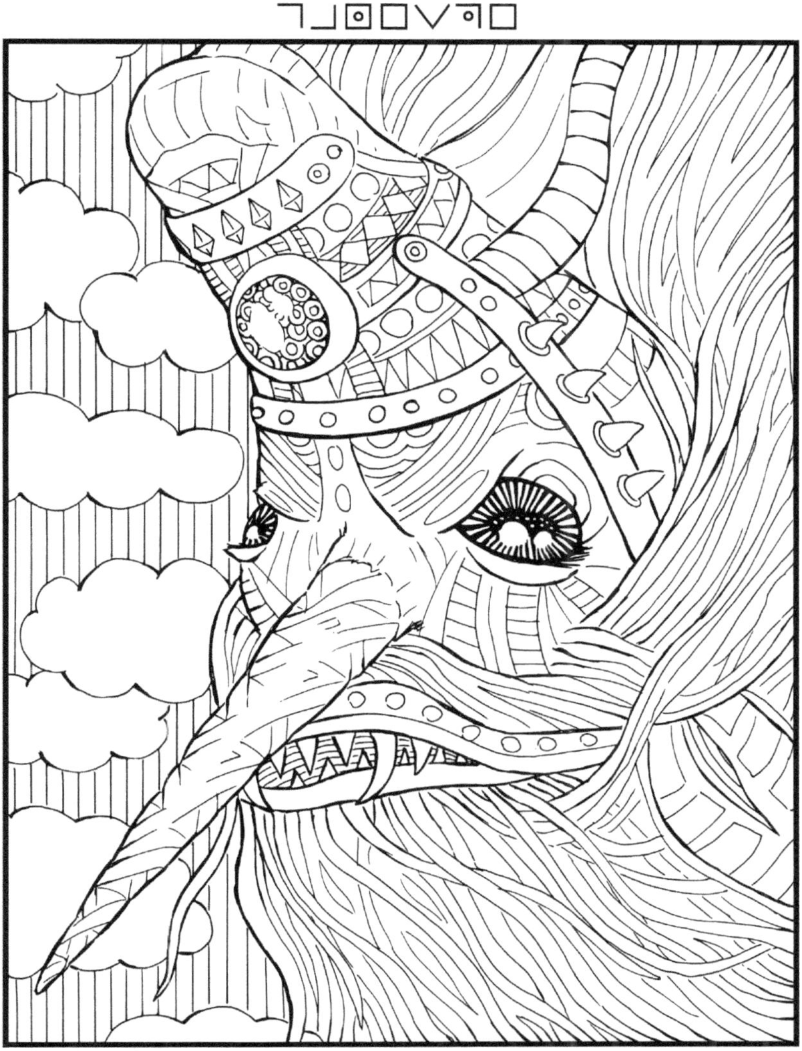

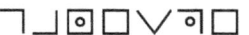

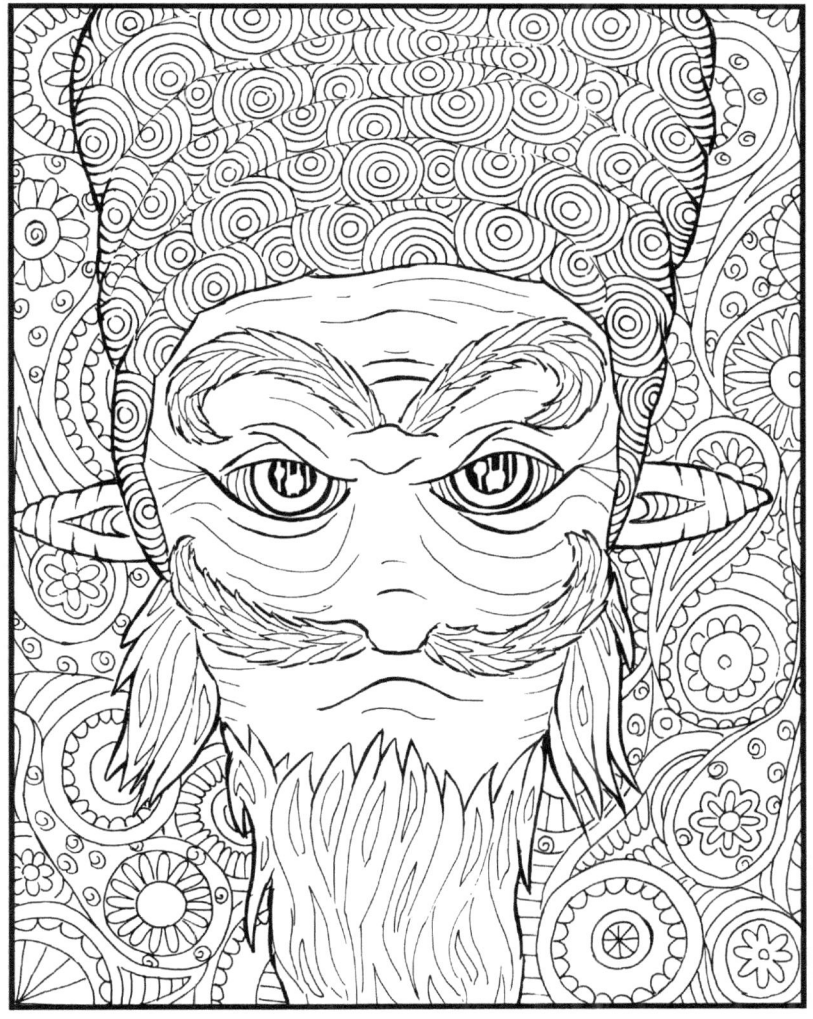

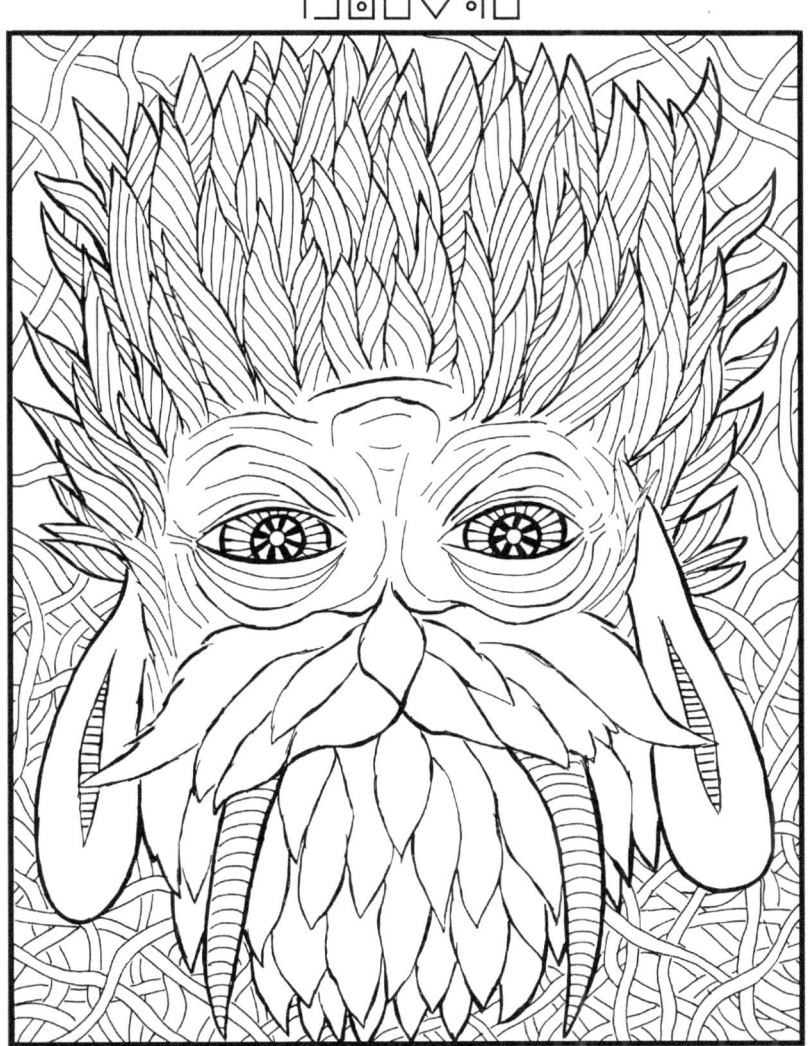

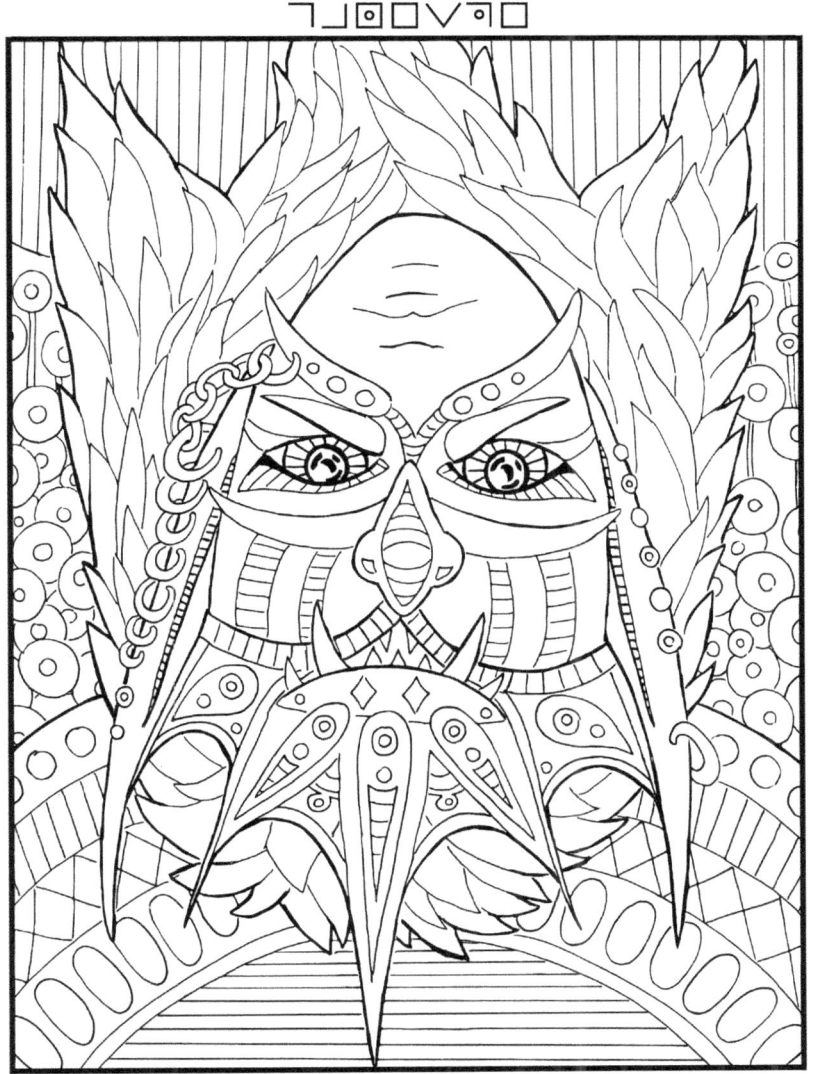

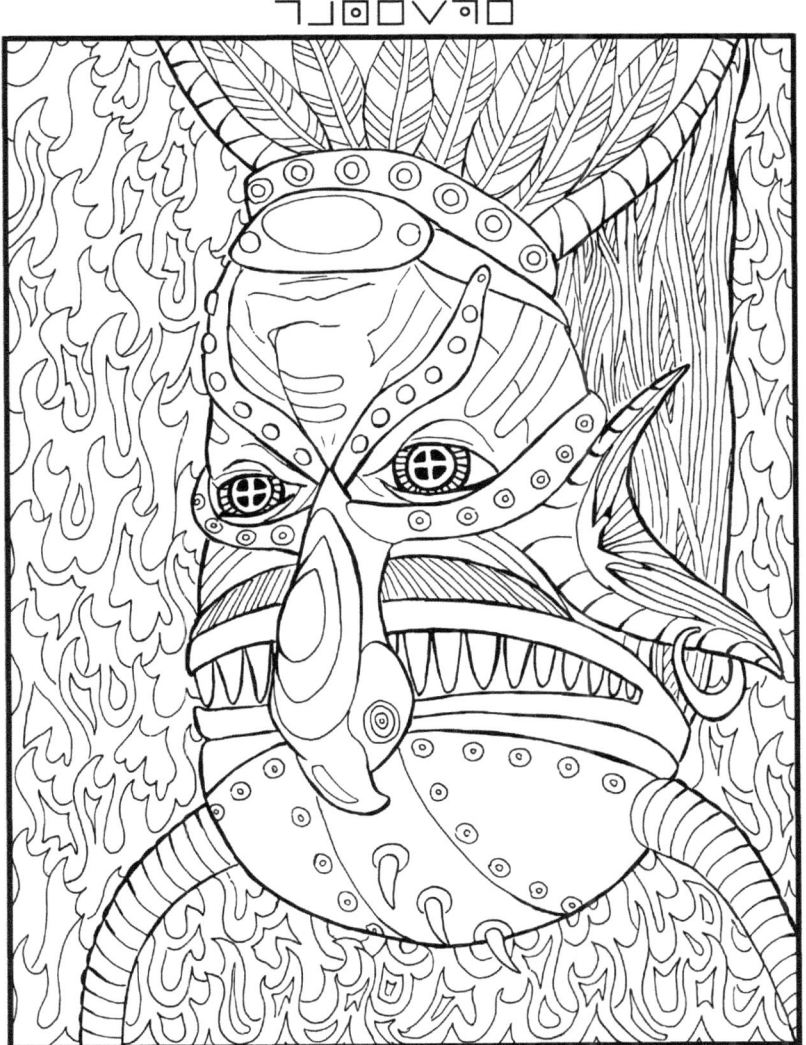

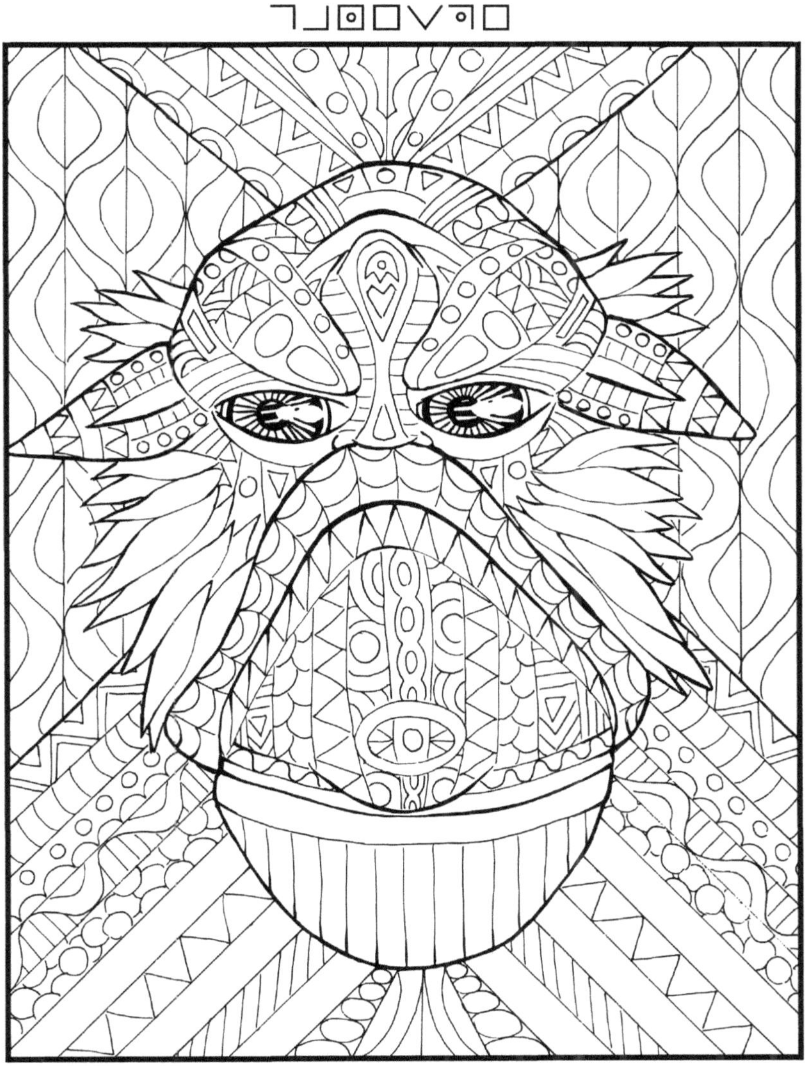

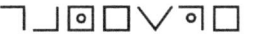

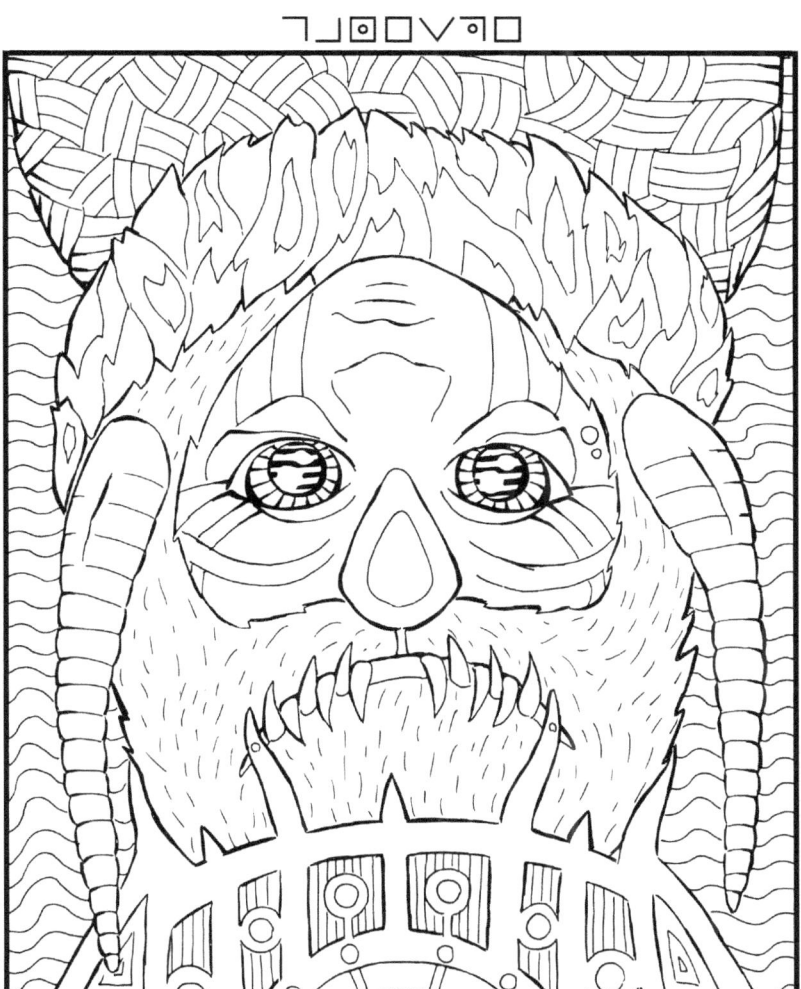

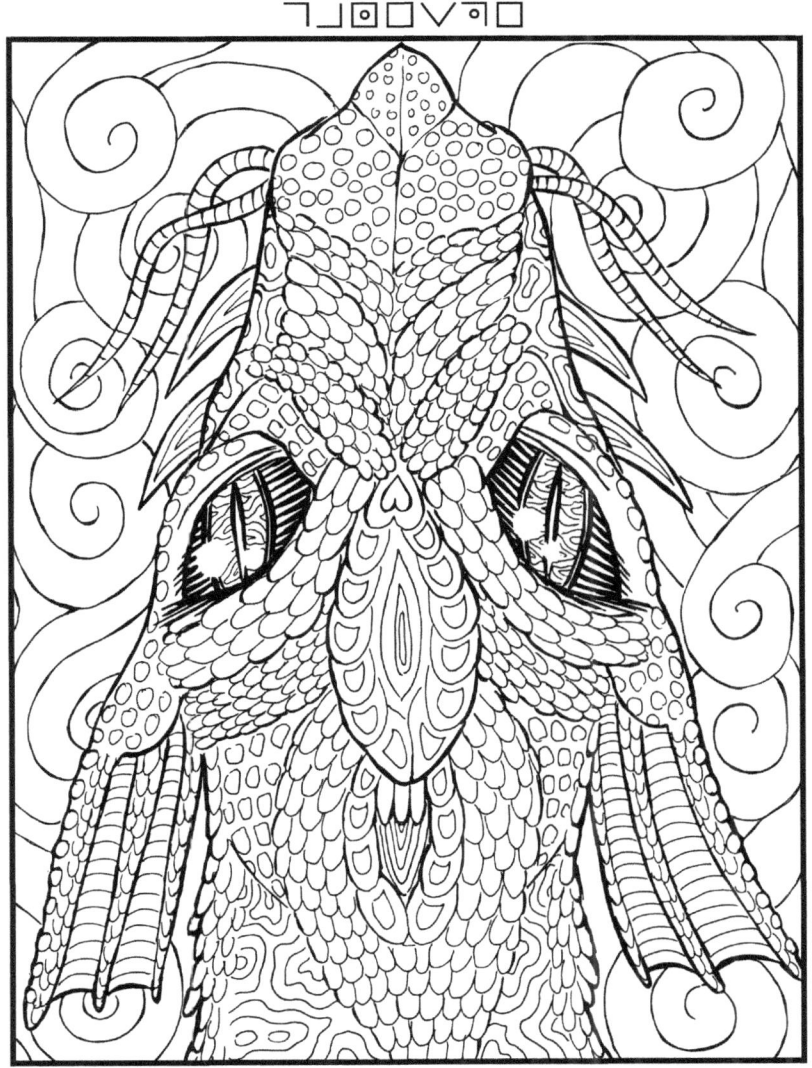

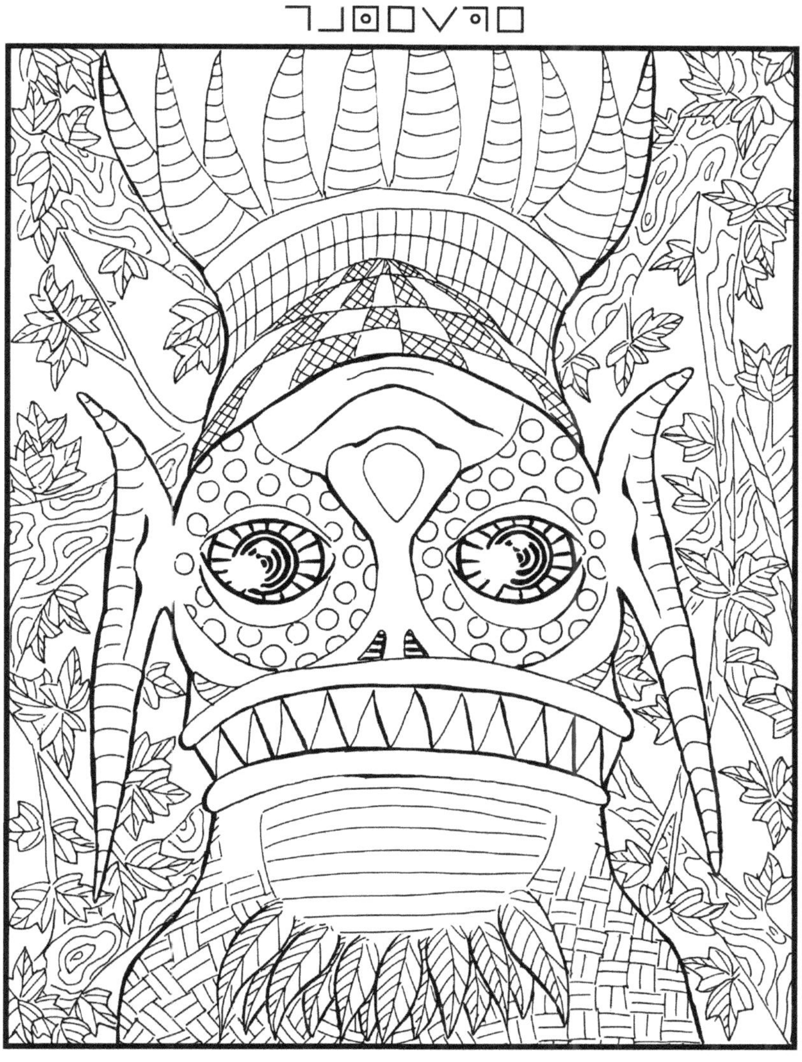

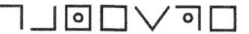

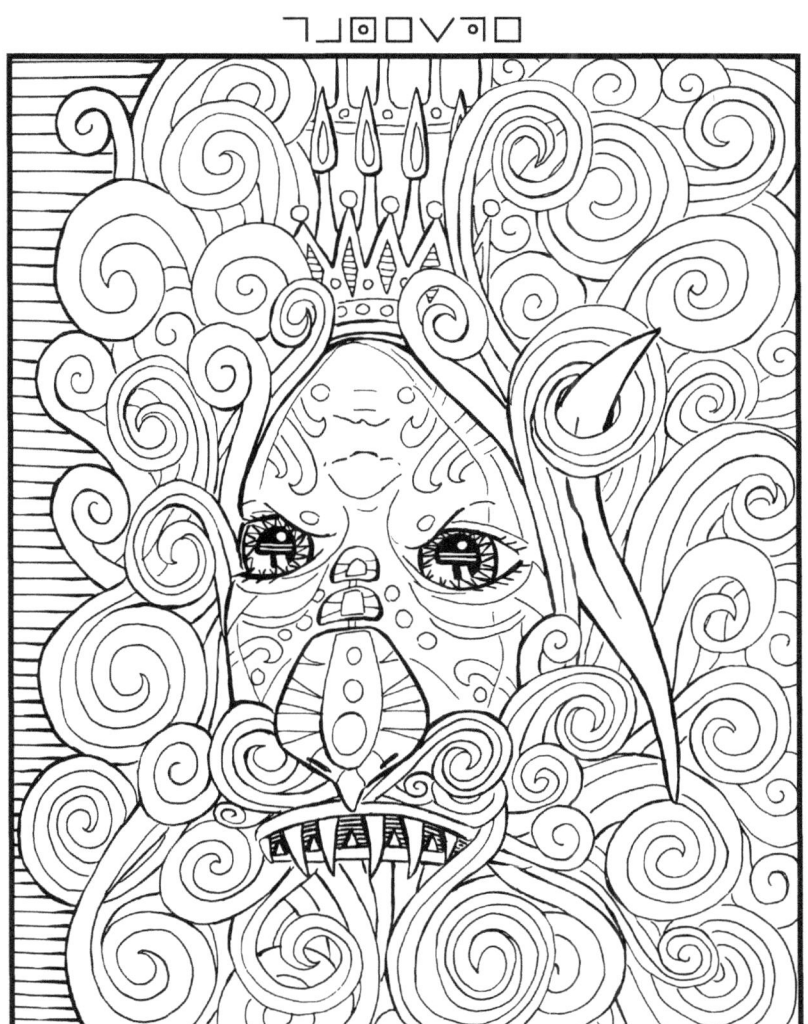

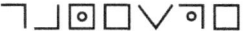

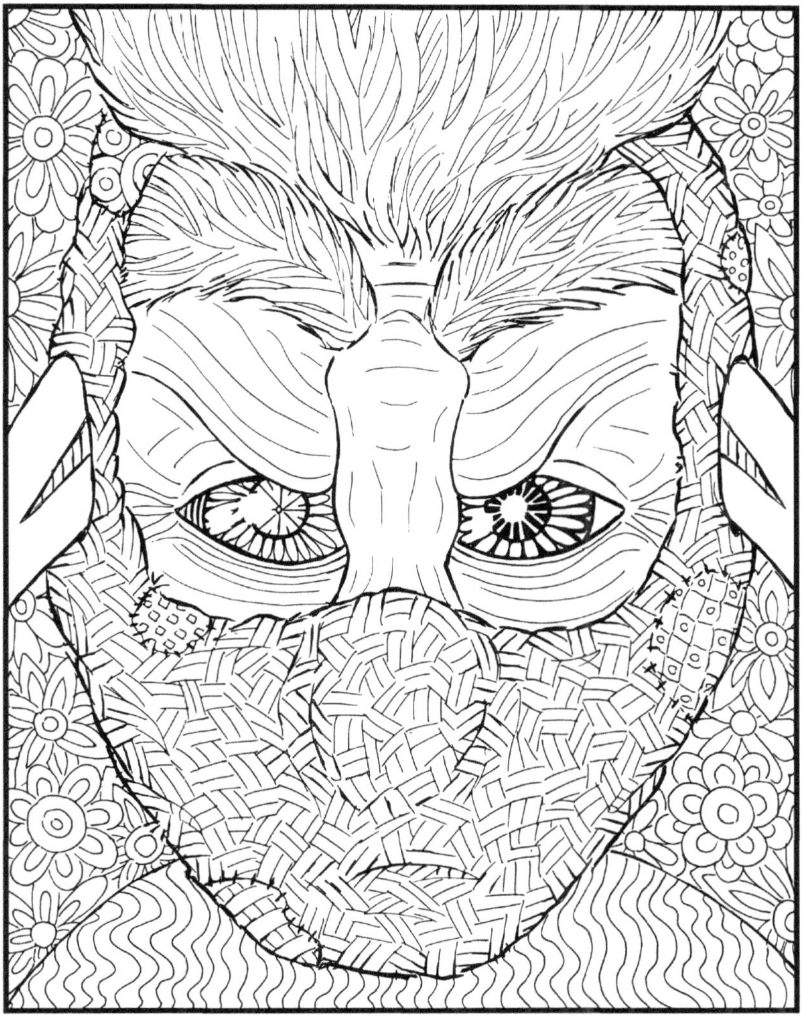

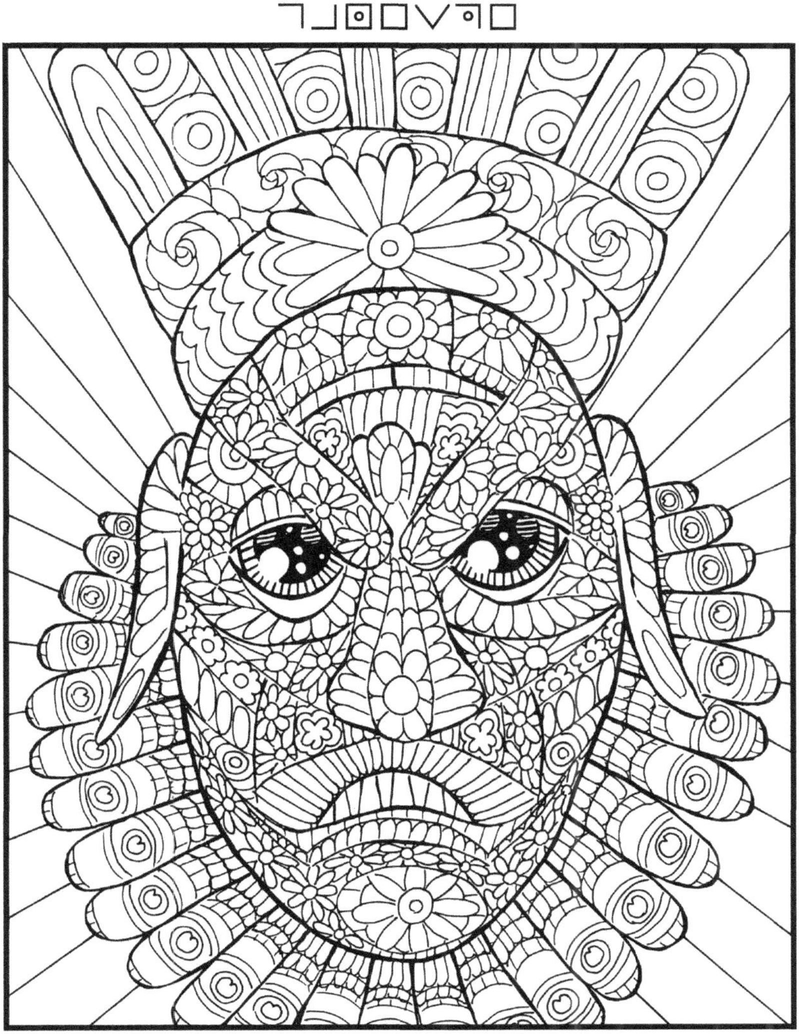

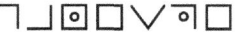

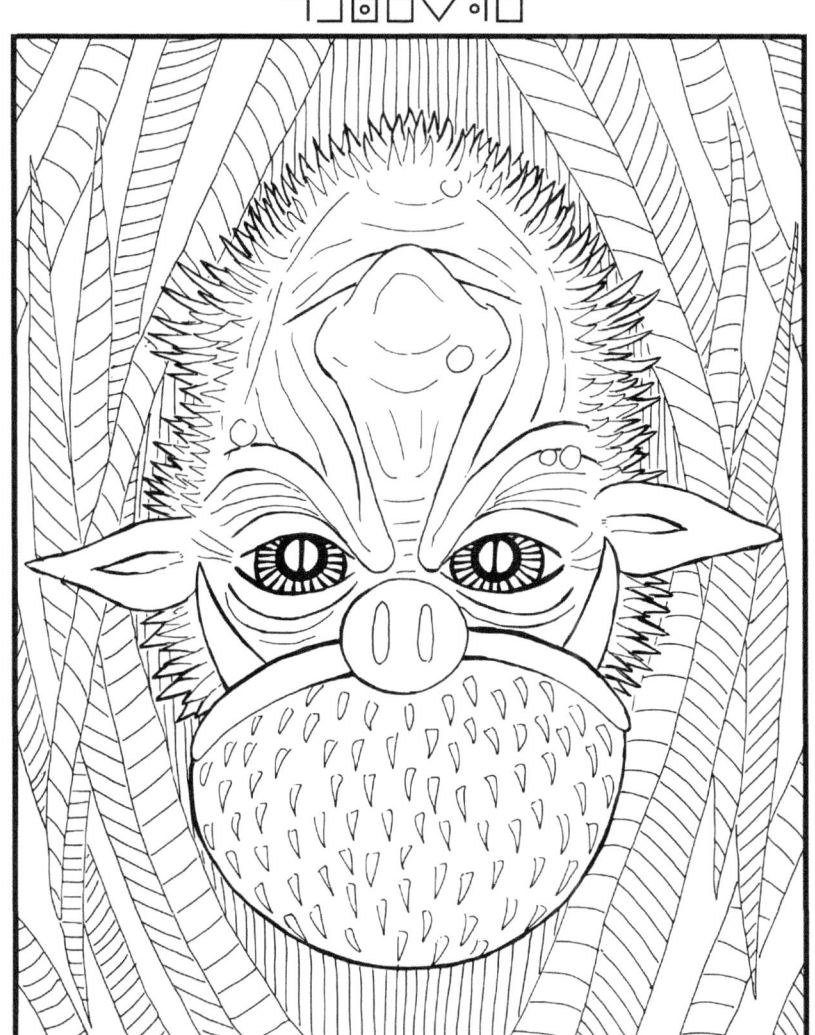

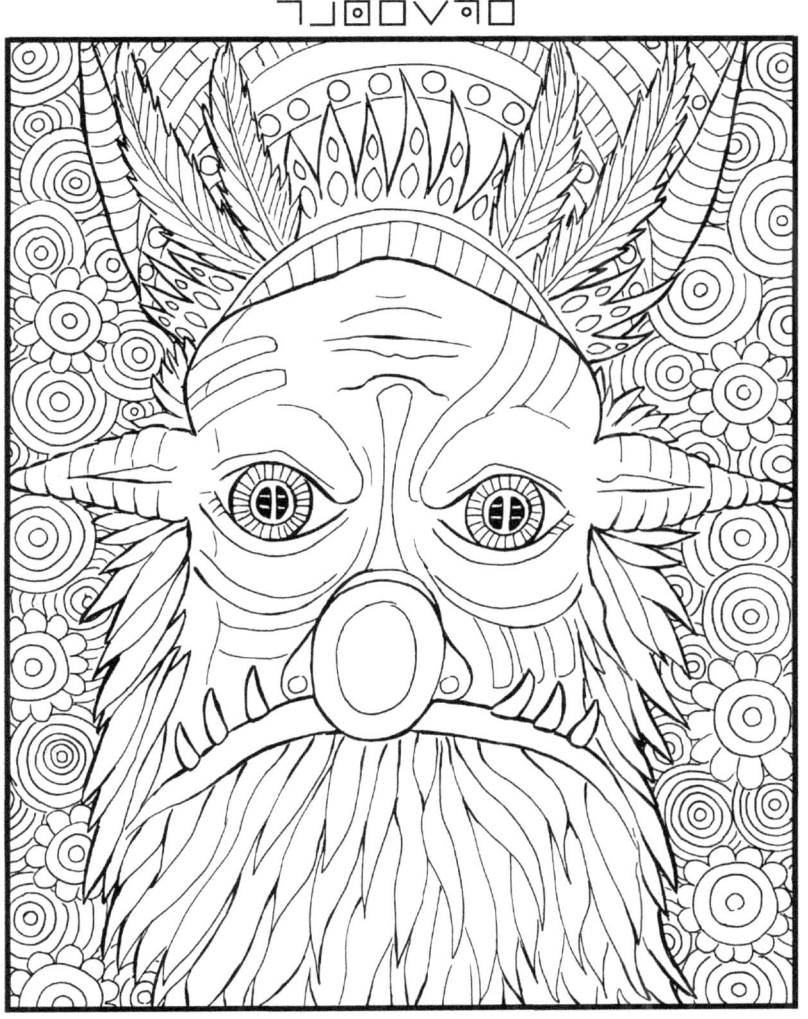

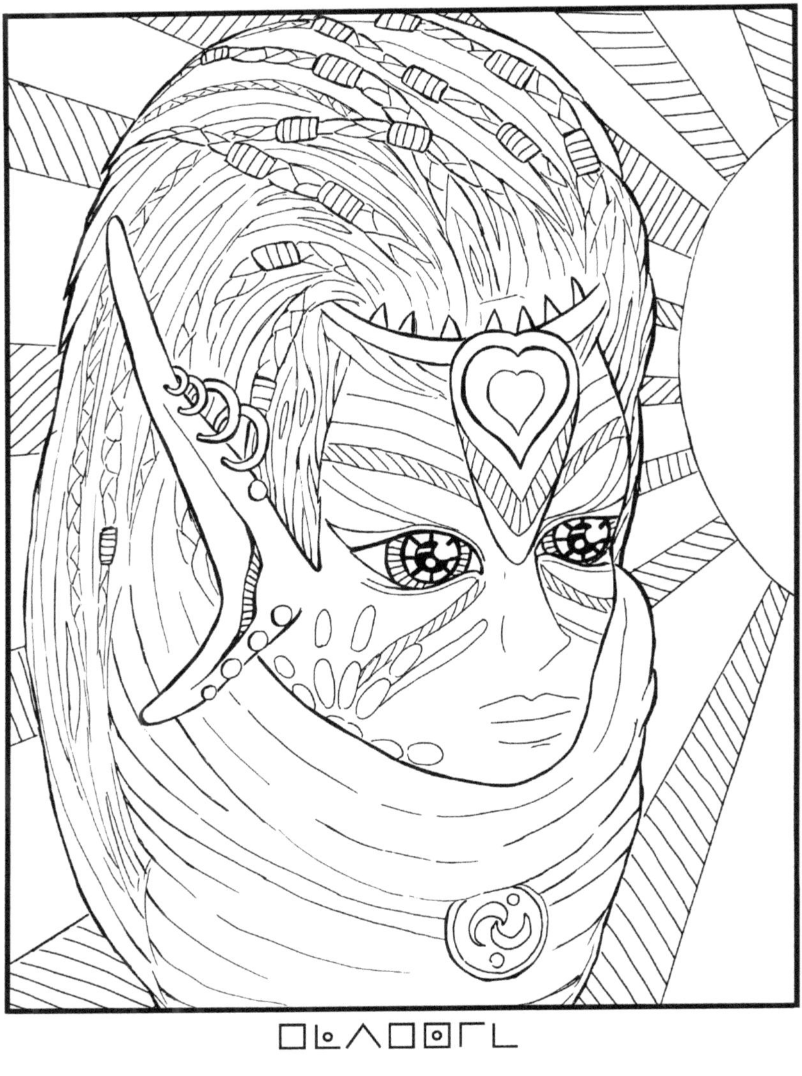

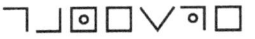

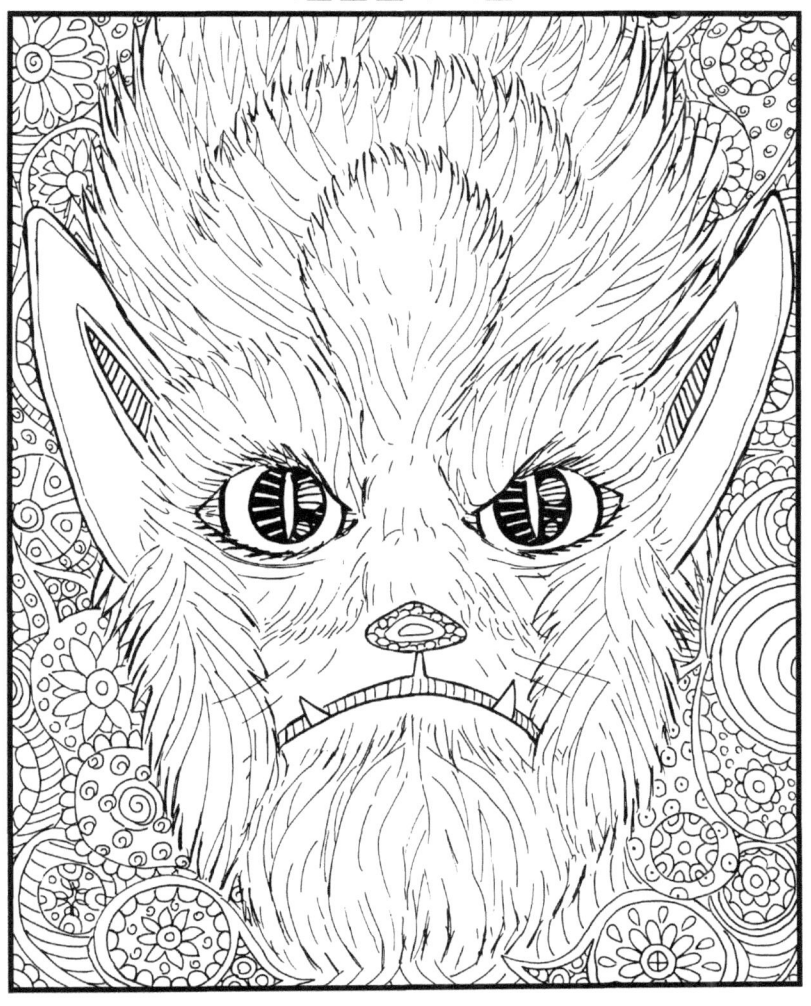

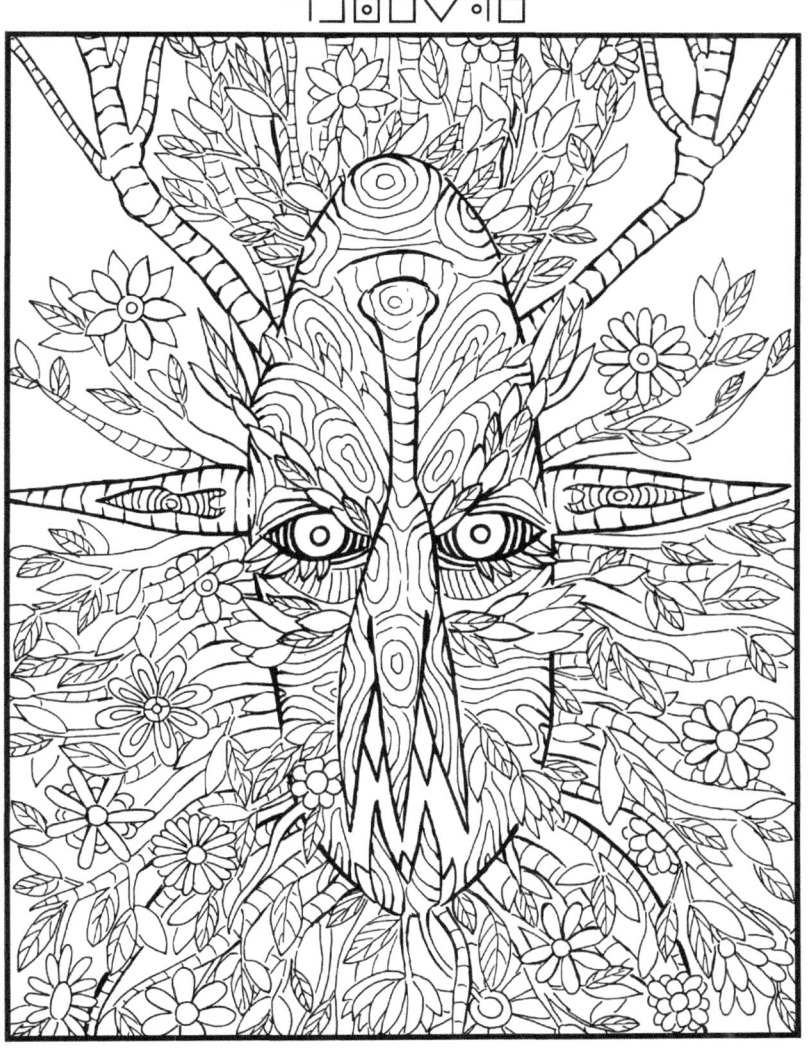

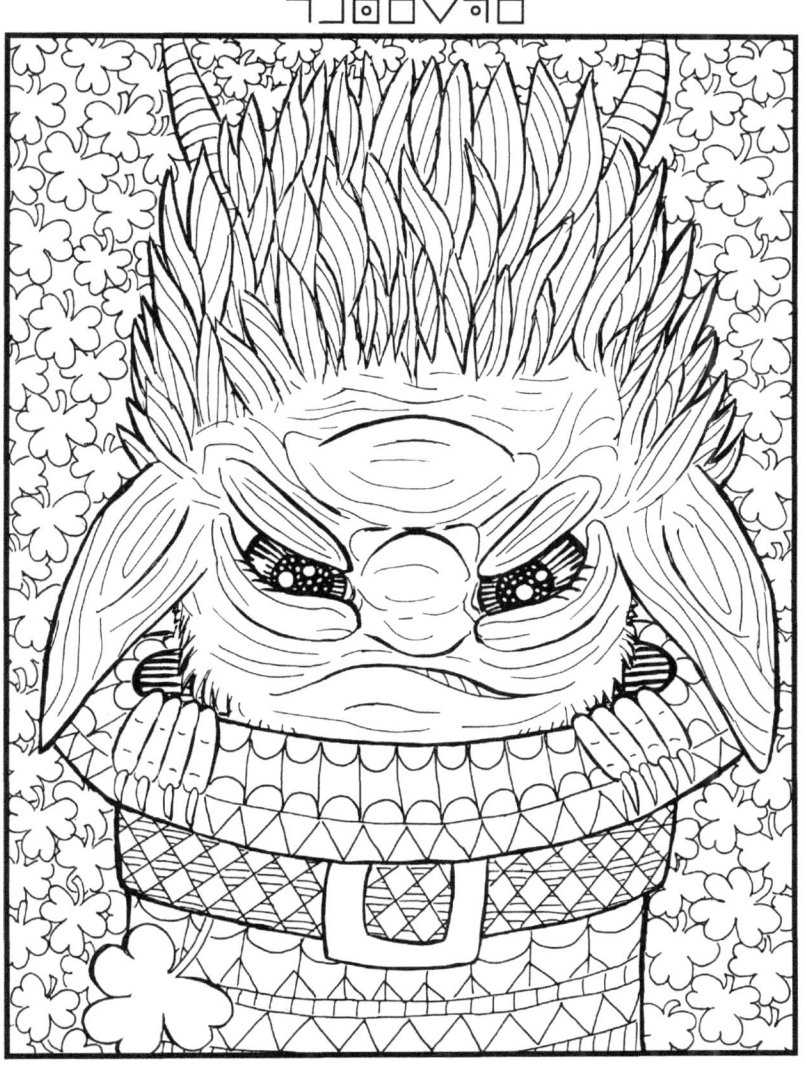

TEST AREA

Use this page to test out your colors and the way
your media interacts with the paper.

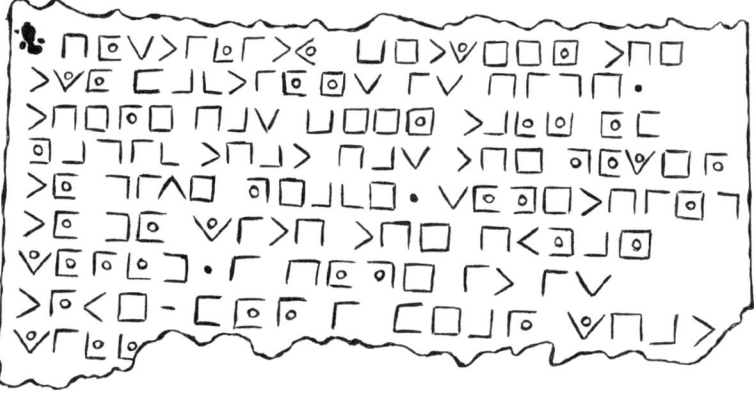

For free coloring pages and artwork by me ('Trick) visit

www.TricksPlace.com

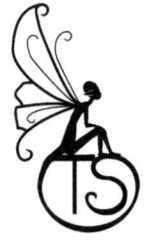

Also check out the "Multiview Illusions Coloring Book"
by 'Trick Slattery:

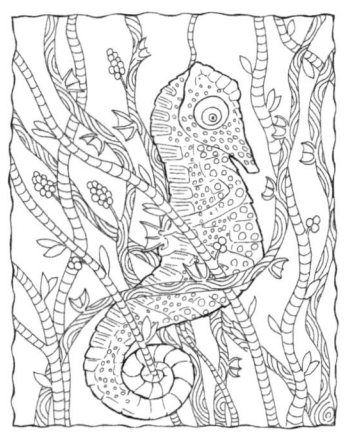

SEAHORSE or CHAMELEON?

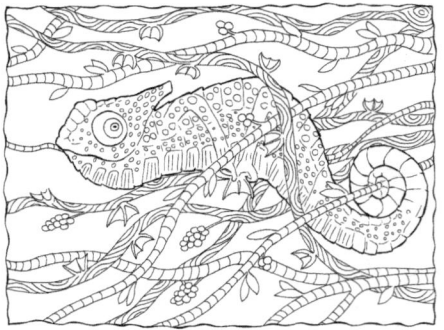

If you've enjoyed this coloring book please leave me a nice
review on Amazon! Your help getting this book noticed will also
allow me to create other unique coloring books.

And don't forget to connect with me at TricksPlace.com, follow
me on facebook.com/tricksplace/ and also join the facebook
group dedicated to sharing colored in pages from my books or
website: facebook.com/groups/TricksPlaceColoring/

#tricksplace #fantasyflipcoloring